IF I GIVE MY SOUL

IF I GIVE MY SOUL

FAITH BEHIND BARS IN RIO DE JANEIRO

ANDREW JOHNSON

OXFORD
UNIVERSITY PRESS

OXFORD
UNIVERSITY PRESS

Oxford University Press is a department of the University of Oxford. It furthers
the University's objective of excellence in research, scholarship, and education
by publishing worldwide. Oxford is a registered trade mark of Oxford University
Press in the UK and certain other countries.

Published in the United States of America by Oxford University Press
198 Madison Avenue, New York, NY 10016, United States of America.

© Oxford University Press 2017

CIP data is on file at the Library of Congress
ISBN 978-0-19-023899-5 (pbk)
ISBN 978-0-19-023898-8 (hbk)

For my wife, Rosane

CONTENTS

ACKNOWLEDGMENTS

First, I would like to thank the Templeton Foundation for a research grant that allowed me to live in Brazil and conduct the fieldwork for this project. I would also like to thank Penny Edgell, my graduate school advisor, for her intellectual contribution to the project and for the support she provided since I first presented the idea to her months before I started graduate school.

The manuscript for the book took shape during a one-year post-doctoral fellowship at Princeton University's Center for the Study of Religion. It was a privilege to be able to present unfinished ideas in seminars, and the input I received provided direction I sorely needed at the time. I finished the manuscript as a member of the Center for Religion and Civic Culture (CRCC) at the University of Southern California. This book has been shaped by my colleagues at CRCC and their vision to "engage scholars and build communities." I thank Richard Flory for being both a mentor and a formidable Whiffle Ball opponent.

I would like to acknowledge my loving wife, Rosane, for her unwavering support and for the countless hours she selflessly contributed to this project. She visited me inside of prison, endured grinding commutes on public transportation to accompany me on research-site visits, transcribed dozens of interviews in Portuguese, and encouraged me to press on when I didn't think I could write another word. Thank you, Rosane, I love you.

My family has also been a source of support throughout the years I have been thinking, researching, and writing this book. I could not be more thankful for their love and support. My mom encouraged me to stray from the beaten path, my brother reminded me that it was worth it when I started to doubt, and my dad read every paragraph I put in front of him. The fingerprints of my conversations with him are all over this book.

I am fortunate to have skilled and generous friends who contributed to the project in their own unique ways. Nick Shindo Street did a wonderful job editing the manuscript and elevating what was often pedestrian writing into something much better. I wrote the book on a computer that Noah Day gave to me when mine was stolen and I was stuck. Bob Brenneman became a good friend through a shared research interest and his work deeply influenced my research. Ryan Patch and I made a documentary film about faith inside of Rio de Janeiro's prisons: working with him transformed the way I looked at the data I had collected for this book.

All of the institutional and personal support would have been for naught if I could not have gained access to the prisons and jails in Brazil. I would like to thank the APAC (Association for Protection and Assistance of Convicts) administration for trusting me to spend two weeks living inside of their prison as a recuperando. Partnering with Rio de Paz in Rio changed the trajectory of this project and I am grateful to the staff and volunteers for the way they embraced me and contributed to the research. I was granted access to these places in large part because of the goodwill and trust they established with both the inmates and institutional administration before I arrived. I am particularly thankful to Antonio Carlos Costa for his friendship and for his example of how to live with both passion and purpose.

Finally, I would like to thank the inmates I met inside of the jails and prisons in Rio de Janeiro and Minas Gerais. Thank you for your hospitality, patience, vulnerability, trust, and conversation. The dignified lives that many of you fashioned out of miserable circumstances left a lasting mark on my life, and I hope this book does them justice.

INTRODUCTION

Carlos was born into a poor family. His parents drank hard. When he was almost eight, and the alcohol-fueled beatings became more than he could bear, he started to sleep on the streets. In downtown Rio de Janeiro, he found a group of boys who had escaped similar situations. They supported themselves with begging and petty theft. Carlos chuckled as he told me about that time in his life. "I used to go to the beach, Copacabana and Ipanema, and rob *gringos* like you," he said.

Both of his parents died, and after six hard years on the streets Carlos went back to his neighborhood. Fourteen years old and all alone, he joined the narco-gang that controlled his community. He took orders well and was fearless during armed robberies, so he rose quickly. After seven years, he was giving orders instead of taking them.

In his early twenties, he pulled off a brazen armed robbery, which netted what was equivalent to nearly US$20,000 in cash. He couldn't deposit the money in a bank or stash it in his home, so he carried it with him. But $20,000 is a hard secret to keep. Within a week, a neighbor tipped off two police officers, who then ambushed Carlos outside a motel. They didn't bother with an arrest, but they took the cash. The informant, who likely got a cut of the haul, had violated the gang's law against speaking to the police. As Carlos said, "If you 'rat' on your comrade, your sentence is death."

Once again, secrets were hard to keep in Carlos's neighborhood, and he soon knew the informant's identity. "They brought him to me, and, possessed by demons, I took the life of that young man," he said. After the killing, the police found Carlos again, but this time they made an arrest, and shortly after he was sentenced to prison for murder.

Carlos settled into prison life. He had lived in worse places. His life had been a series of difficult transitions—childhood, street life, the gang, and now prison. After more than a decade behind bars, he would make another transition, this time by converting to Pentecostal Christianity.

It began as he sat in his cell listening to the singing and rhythmic clapping of a group of inmates gathered in the patio for a Pentecostal worship service. He had heard hundreds, maybe thousands of these services from inside his cell, but Pentecostalism, or any religion, had never interested him. Prison was not Carlos's first exposure to Pentecostalism. The *favela* where he was born and later worked for the gang was full of Pentecostal churches, but to him they had been only background noise.

"There were four or five churches, even an Assembly of God in my community," he said. "But to be honest I didn't even like *crentes* [Portuguese for believers]. I thought they were crazy. I thought they were psychos because they walked around in the hot sun dressed just like I am right now." We were sitting inside a Pentecostal church on the outskirts of Rio de Janeiro and as he spoke he pointed to his gray suit, blue tie, and freshly pressed white shirt. He smiled to acknowledge the irony.

"The truth is, I was already tired of the life I was living. I didn't know who to turn to and I found myself desperate, in a dead end. I was looking for something that would embrace me, something that would help me. I saw the brothers from the church and I saw their sincerity and I saw their commitment to God. I went to see if God would truly set me free. Because I did not believe in liberation, I did not believe in transformation."

So Carlos put out his cigarette, left his cell, and walked toward the edge of the worship service. He couldn't recall everything that happened that day, but he remembered that the pastor, an inmate himself, was reading from the book of John: "Then you will know the truth, and the truth will set you free." The message of redemption and personal salvation resonated with Carlos, and when the inmate pastor asked if anyone wanted to give their soul to Christ, Carlos lifted his hand. The pastor cut through the crowd to Carlos and placed his hands on Carlos's head. He began a fervent prayer in a staccato cadence that grew louder and louder until Carlos fell to the ground.

"When I finally got up, I felt really light," Carlos said. "I stood up as if I were another person. I believe that the legion of demons that was in me all left on that day."

His fellow inmates helped Carlos to his feet and once he shook his head to regain his senses, he reached into his pocket, grabbed his pack of cigarettes, and gave it to another inmate. Giving away the cigarettes was his first act as a practicing Pentecostal, because *crentes* are expected to live a certain way inside of prison and they do not smoke. After making a public commitment to God in front of his cellmates, Carlos made other lifestyle changes in order to adhere to the strict expectations of a Pentecostal inside prison.

"I started to praise the name of Jesus Christ my savior right there in prison, you know. I stopped with all that smoking and snorting cocaine. I used to use prostitutes, but I stopped that, too."

But Carlos's conversion meant more than simply removing vices from his life. After the prayer that literally knocked him off his feet, he formally left the gang he had served for over ten years and joined the inmate-led church.

"The gang let me leave because they could see the sincerity in my heart. They could see that it wasn't lies leaving my lips, and that the tears rolling down my cheeks were not lies."

Released from prison two years later, Carlos reentered society as a Pentecostal. With a Bible under his arm, he caught a bus outside the prison door and rode it to his old neighborhood. When he arrived, Carlos's gang colleagues offered him work that would pay ten times what he could have earned in the job market.

"I had to refuse," he said, "because I had accepted Jesus. I accepted Jesus in prison."

He went to a Pentecostal church whose members had visited him in prison. For a month, he slept under a bridge and went to the church for the worship services and a hot meal. When the church offered Carlos a place to sleep, he moved into a room reserved for men leaving prison or a gang. When I met Carlos he had been living at the church for nearly two years. He called it his home and would greet the worshippers at the door before the nightly services.

Carlos is one of literally thousands of men living in Rio de Janeiro who converted to Pentecostal Christianity inside the city's prisons or participated in a prison church while incarcerated. Prison Pentecostalism represents a hidden but important part of the Pentecostal movement that has swept through Rio de Janeiro and much of Brazil over the past three decades. This book responds to a simple research question, "Why is Pentecostalism so widely practiced inside Rio de Janeiro's prisons and jails?"

There are many ways to answer that question. One is theological. To the believer, Pentecostalism provides an answer to humanity's most persistent questions: Where do we come from, and where are we going when we die?

But this book is a sociological, not theological, study of Pentecostalism. While recognizing the importance of theology in the success of any religion, I avoid theological interpretations of the Pentecostalism I studied. For example, when I report that Carlos told me that "the legion of demons that was in me all left on that day," I do not try to explain his description of the event by presenting an alternate explanation of what was *really* going on. I will also not use his account as evidence that there are supernatural entities actively intervening in individuals' lives. My goal is neither to affirm nor dismantle the theological underpinnings of Pentecostalism. Rather, the intent and scope of this study is to analyze the social world in and around Rio's prisons to explain why Pentecostalism flourishes there.

Pentecostalism is practiced most frequently in Rio's *favelas* and peripheral neighborhoods from whence come most of the city's prison inmates. Therefore, the prison population is primarily composed of individuals in the sociodemographic group most likely to practice the faith. But stating that Pentecostalism is strong inside prison because prisoners are poor and therefore more likely to be Pentecostal does not contribute much to research on the relationship between Pentecostalism and the poor, nor does it add to the sociological research on prison subculture.

The Pentecostalism practiced inside prison, what I will call Prison Pentecostalism, uniquely reflects the prison environment and is not simply a replication of the faith practiced on the streets. An answer that depends solely on sociodemographic data will be incomplete because prisoners are being held against their will and must deal with a set of hardships unique to their incarceration, what Gresham Sykes (1958) called the "pains of imprisonment."

Pentecostalism addresses those pains by providing a tight-knit community for believers, protection for vulnerable members, and access to scarce resources inside the cellblocks. It clearly helps inmates cope with the brutal realities of incarceration. For example, immediately after his conversion, Carlos became part of a community of Pentecostal inmates who shared their limited resources and protected each other from the violence that lurks just beneath the surface of prison life, helping him survive his last few years in prison.

But framing Pentecostalism as simply a coping mechanism does not capture what I believe represents the heart of its success behind bars: dignity. In this book, I argue that Pentecostalism resonates so deeply with inmates like Carlos because it offers a belief system and a set of practices that enable an inmate to embody a new, publicly recognizable identity and a platform for prisoners to live a moral and dignified life both in prison and after they are released.

I contend that living with dignity goes beyond simply coping with stigma or difficult circumstances. Carlos, for example, was born on the stigmatized margins of society and has stayed there most of his life. As a kid living on the streets he learned how to dodge the rolled-up newspapers swung at his head by shopkeepers who didn't want him close to their stores. On the steps of Candelária Church in downtown Rio de Janeiro, he slept with one eye open for the murderous vigilante groups tasked with permanently removing children like him from public spaces.[1]

Throughout his life, he had very little substantial contact with anyone who was not living on the margins of the city. He barely went to school and when he left the streets his work in the gang-controlled narcotics traffic kept him sequestered in and around his neighborhood's drug-distribution points that are hidden from the rest of the city.

Carlos's only meaningful interactions with Rio's middle and upper classes occurred when he left his hillside neighborhood to commit armed robberies. Those interactions came to a screeching halt when he was incarcerated for murder. Carlos's trajectory was one that many other poor, dark-skinned young men in Rio de Janeiro have traveled: impoverished household, employment in drug traffic, and eventually prison.

I interviewed Carlos four years after his conversion and two years after his release from prison. I asked him to describe how he currently understood his place in society.

> These days, I am known as a man of God. A long time ago when people talked to me, actually they didn't talk to me, they just waited until I turned my back and walked down the street to say, "Look at that drug trafficker, look at that addict, what a bum." Even if I were painted in gold, people would not look at me. Now they will take a photo with me, ask me to give a word, ask me to pray for them. I don't just feel it; I know that I have value in society. Because before, nobody wanted to be close to me, nobody would walk by my side. Much less invite me into their house to pray. Nobody is going to invite a murderer and drug dealer into their home. Who would do that? But today it is not like that any more, now I am invited. Today they say, "There goes a man of God." ... It is gratifying to hear these things because in the past they didn't even want to look at me.

Carlos knew the pain of living a life without dignity. More than just poverty, he knew what it felt like to see people cross the street when he approached. Life was hard, and conversion to Pentecostalism was not a magic bullet that immediately solved all his problems. It did not launch him into a stable job when he left prison, nor did it lift him out of poverty. When I met Carlos, he had three ill-fitting, second-hand suits, a few ties, and not much else. His grammar and style of speech revealed his minimal education to anyone he met. Even though the suit he wore and the Bible he carried identified him as a practicing Pentecostal, he still remained a member of Rio de Janeiro's "killable people."

In spite of the lack of upward mobility, when I spoke with him, he was proud of the life he was living and the "man of God" he had become. Proud enough to return to the drug dens and prisons where he once lived and worked to preach a message of hope. For Carlos, his Pentecostal conversion and identity as a *crente* went beyond coping with the pain of life in prison, the stigma of poverty, and the absence of jobs. For the first time in his life, he could walk with his head held high.

This study of Prison Pentecostalism is based on dozens of interviews with prisoners and former prisoners, inside and outside some of the worst prisons in Rio de Janeiro, as well as on two weeks I spent living in cellblocks in the same conditions as prisoners. Conversations about my methodology almost always elicit some form of the question, "Were you safe?" The short answer is "Yes, I was safe. I made it through without a scratch." Chapter 1 gives a longer, more detailed answer to that question.

Prison is a difficult place to access and a challenging place to conduct fieldwork. I started the research for this book not in Rio de Janeiro but in the neighboring state of Minas Gerais where I spent two weeks living in a prison. I slept in the same cells, ate the same food, and used the same bathrooms as the other prisoners in my cellblock. I spent one week each in two separate prisons and in each I went through the daily routines as if I were incarcerated. Of course, I could have left at almost any time and everyone in my cellblock knew it. But by living there I was able to catch a glimpse of prison life from the inside. I was able to see firsthand the unique emotional hardships of incarceration, the monotonous daily routine. I became familiar with the unwritten rules that are often followed more closely than the formal rules. I was also able to refine my research question and narrow my focus from "religion inside Brazilian prisons" to "Pentecostalism in prisons in Rio de Janeiro."

After those two weeks in prison, I lived in Rio de Janeiro in 2010 collecting qualitative data in the city's jails and prisons, the homes of inmates, the gang-controlled neighborhoods, and the numerous Pentecostal churches in the city. I made subsequent research trips to the city in 2011, 2012, and 2013. In this chapter I will introduce Salgado Jail and Cinza Penitentiary,[2] where I conducted most of my research through participant observation and by interviewing dozens of prisoners. In the neighborhoods surrounding the prisons, I interviewed dozens more former prisoners, like Carlos.

Rio's prison system has a global reputation for violence, injustice, and human rights violations.[3] But even though I had read about these prisons, I had no idea what the term "overcrowded prisons" really meant until I stood inside of a cell built for fifteen people alongside seventy other men. It is difficult to accurately convey the sights, sounds, and smells of those places, but in chapter 1, I will describe the conditions, as well as how I was treated by the inmates, guards, and volunteers who regularly visit.

This book is about Pentecostalism inside prison, but it is also a book about the city of Rio de Janeiro, *a cidade marivilhosa* ("the marvelous city"). In many ways, Rio is a city divided. The social inequality woven into its very fabric rivals that of any other major city in the world. The prisons and the neighborhoods where most of the city's inmates lived before they were arrested share little in common with the picturesque neighborhoods in Rio's famed *zona sul* or the gated and guarded apartment complexes where the middle and upper classes live. A walk through any of Rio's penal facilities, or the socially isolated *favelas*, makes the city's nickname—"the marvelous city"—seem a cruel joke. These places were not featured in the city's successful bids to host the 2014 World Cup or the 2016 Olympic Games, but they are important because they represent the Rio de Janeiro where Carlos and dozens of other men who participated in this project lived their lives.

The first *favelas* started to emerge in Rio de Janeiro in the middle of the nineteenth century, decades before the Golden Law was passed freeing the slaves in Brazil.[4] Ever since these informal communities first sprouted on the hillsides, the Brazilian state has woefully failed to provide residents basic education, healthcare, security, and inclusion into the formal economy. Over the last thirty years, powerful narco-gangs have taken control of these spaces and set up a system of governance referred to as *o poder paralello*, the parallel power. I argue that the prisons are extensions of the *favelas* and marginalized neighborhoods in Rio because like those impoverished areas they are characterized by a weak state presence. Both are governed by narco-gangs, and Pentecostalism plays an integral role in daily life.

To illuminate the consequences of Rio's extreme social inequality I will focus specifically on the homicide rates and number of police killings in Rio de Janeiro. Death comes quickly and violently to thousands of Brazilians in Rio's poor areas, and young, darker-skinned males are disproportionately represented in the city's morgue. The levels of violence in Rio de Janeiro have been among the highest in the world over the last twenty years, but they have elicited little outcry from civil society or the state.

The lack of response to the spectacular violence in Rio de Janeiro is largely because of *who* is being killed. In effect, the people living in the *favelas* and other poor neighborhoods in Rio de Janeiro are treated as less than full citizens. For decades their deaths have been largely tolerated because they are members of Rio's marginalized groups. They are the city's "killable people." Likewise, the inhumane and undignified conditions of the city's prisons have been tolerated because Rio's prisons are not filled with inmates from the middle and upper classes. They are jammed beyond capacity with "killable people."

As mentioned earlier, before I set foot inside a Brazilian prison my interest was broad. My initial plan was to study religion inside prison. I did not have a particular faith in mind. Once I started to spend time inside prisons, I realized that Pentecostal Christianity was by far the most widely practiced faith behind bars. Catholicism, Macumba, *Espiritismo*, or any other faith practice was a distant second. On one hand, Pentecostalism's success among inmates should not have come as a surprise because it is the dominant faith in the neighborhoods described in chapter 2. This is the demographic answer to the research question. In chapter 3, I conceptualize Pentecostalism as the "faith of the killable people" and describe the relationship between the Pentecostal church and its leaders, the city's impoverished communities, and the narco-gangs. Pentecostal church members, specifically pastors, have earned tremendous respect among the residents of the city's marginalized spaces as well as among the gangs that control these areas. For example, gangs generally allow members to leave if they join a Pentecostal church as long as their conversion and subsequent practice are deemed genuine.

Pastor Antonio Carlos Costa, founder of the human rights group Rio de Paz, told me, "There is not a Pentecostal church in a poor neighborhood in Rio de Janeiro that does not have at least one converted drug trafficker." The relationship between Pentecostal churches and the narco-gangs is characterized by mutual respect. The churches do not condone the gang's drug traffic, violence, and hedonism, but they treat gang members as people worthy of redemption. Another important part of this relationship is that the Pentecostals do not challenge the gang's power in their neighborhoods. The gangs in turn command their members to treat the church members and pastors with respect and to acknowledge their authority in the community. I heard numerous accounts of gang members providing assistance to churches when they held public street revivals in their neighborhoods, and I personally observed church leaders and gang members working together to address community issues.

Chapter 4 is an inside look at the inmate-led Pentecostal prison churches that represent the organizational center of Prison Pentecostalism. Drawing on data I collected at Salgado Jail and Cinza Penitentiary, I describe the autonomous prison churches like the one Carlos joined. These churches, not formally affiliated with a denomination or a para-church prison ministry, are led by inmate pastors, deacons, secretaries, and worship leaders. Created inside prison walls, they have been uniquely shaped by their immediate context and are not exact replications of the Pentecostal churches outside.

I will argue that one of the reasons the prison churches not only survive but also thrive in this difficult space is because in many ways they resemble the prison gangs in structure and function. Both gang and prison church claim part of the prison as their own, each implements and enforces a set of rules for their members, and each provides a strong identity to participants and offers them protection and community.

In chapter 5, I take a "lived religion" approach and build on the work of scholars who have chosen to focus on the embodied practice and emotional content of religion (Edgell 2012; Tavory and Winchester 2012; Winchester 2008). I argue that practice is important when studying religion from a sociological perspective, especially in the prison context. There is an inherent skepticism about "jailhouse religion," so instead of trying to ascertain if the inmates really "believed" in the theological tenants of Pentecostalism, I focused on their practice, or what they did inside prison.

One of the most consistent critiques of Pentecostals has been that they focus on saving individual souls while ignoring structural injustices that oppress people and groups here on earth. There were certainly moments during the fieldwork when the data seemed to support this argument. In general, the Pentecostal volunteers directed their efforts at converting inmates and sometimes appeared oblivious or unconcerned about the blatant human rights abuses inside the prison. With very few exceptions, the volunteers did not try to press the government for prison reform or protest against a police force that has killed over one thousand people every year for more than a decade. There has been a wave of protests throughout Brazil over the resources spent to host the World Cup and Olympic Games, but not about the treatment of the poor or the incredible rates of homicides and police killings in urban Brazil. Though the neighborhoods that are most adversely affected by this violence are full of Pentecostal churches, there has not been anything like a Brazilian version of the #blacklivesmatter campaign that has come as a result of police killings in the American cities of Ferguson, New York, Cleveland, Los Angeles, and other places.

Most of these critiques against Pentecostals are built on their apparent lack of traditional political participation, yet I argue in chapter 6 that it is a mistake to claim that the actions of Pentecostals in Rio de

Janeiro's prisons do not constitute political action. I suggest an alternative paradigm: that their persistent presence inside the prisons and jails is a political act with political consequences. That presence gives substance to their message that inmates are people of value and worthy of redemption. It flies in the face of the notion that the men inside prison are expendable or killable. I use three examples of Pentecostal responses to state violence, or the threat of state violence, inside prison to introduce a "politics of presence" as a way to understand Pentecostal political action in Rio's prisons.

CHAPTER I

INTO THE "BELLY OF THE BEAST"

I felt glued to the bench in the central plaza of a town in Minas Gerais, Brazil, and unsettled by the growing knot in my stomach. A middle-aged man selling electric beard trimmers out of a ragged cardboard box sat down next to me to rest. Neither of us spoke as we watched a street preacher punctuate his sermon by stabbing the air with a dog-eared Bible. Three weeks prior, I had asked to spend a week inside this town's prison, sleeping in the cells and living as if I were one of the inmates. I wanted to see prison life from the inside. But as I sat there on the bench, I felt like a kid on the edge of a cold swimming pool, thinking that if he waits just a little longer the water will warm up.

The street preacher finished his sermon, the beard-trimmer salesman left the bench, and I, too, decided that it was time to move. I grabbed the bag that held my clothes and toiletries and waved to a driver sitting on the hood of his taxi. We drove to the outskirts, where asphalt transitions into gravel, and arrived at the city's prison, which is wedged between the cemetery and the landfill. Not prime real estate and not subtle symbolism.

I paid the fare, knocked on the prison door, and ten minutes later, I had a pillow, blanket, and a set of sheets in my hands. My contact at the prison gave me a few instructions and we walked together through three sets of heavy iron doors that kept the inmates in and the public out. We arrived at what would be my cell for seven days and nights, and I was given a bunk and a single shelf on which to place my belongings. The prison official asked if I had any other questions. I couldn't think of any so he patted my shoulder, flashed a thumbs-up, and told me that he would see me in a week. Left alone, I put the sheets on my bed, folded my blanket, and wondered who was staying in the other three beds. With my bed made and supplies arranged, I stepped out of the cell and started the fieldwork.

TOURING THE BELLY

Loïc Wacquant (2001) lamented that over the last twenty years, social science research on prisons had shifted from ethnographic studies in the prison yards toward quantitative analyses of large-scale data sets. Wacquant was concerned that as the United States embraced mass incarceration and locked up an unprecedented number of Americans, the daily lives of inmates were becoming increasingly mysterious. He warned that "ethnography of the prison in the United States is not merely an endangered species but a virtually extinct one" (385). Quantitative social science studies on prisons have been tremendously useful in illuminating the frightening consequences of mass incarceration in the United States and other countries (Manza and Uggen 2006; Tonry and Farrington 2005; Western 2006). But Wacquant argues that going into the "belly of the beast"—entering the prison itself—is an essential component of prison studies and he implored social science researchers to return to ethnographic fieldwork.

Wacquant attempted to answer his own call by taking a guided tour of the Los Angeles County Jail. As the guards accompanied him through the facility, his senses were assaulted by the noise, filth, absence of natural light, and disproportionate racial composition of the inmate population. Wacquant's visit to the jail shook him. After he finished, he wrote, "I am numb coming out of this long afternoon inside MCJ (Men's Central Jail) and I drive silently straight to the beach [of Santa Monica] to wallow in the fresh air and wade in the waves, as if to 'cleanse' myself of all I've seen, heard, and sensed. I feel so bad, like scrambled eggs" (381).

I concur that being physically present in a prison, even for just a few hours, is an intense experience that exposes the realities of mass incarceration. But prison tours, like the one that left Wacquant feeling like scrambled eggs, are problematic and unlikely to reveal the nuances of prison life (Piché and Walby 2010). Tours may be the only avenue for social science researchers to gain entrance to penal facilities, but they are short and highly controlled (and possibly manipulated) by prison administrators, and much of the contact with the inmates and guards occurs on what would classify as "front stage" interaction (Goffman 1956).

While I was working out the methodology for this project, I took a guided tour of the Louisiana State Penitentiary, or Angola Prison, as it is more commonly known. Angola is a unique place. First, there is an unprecedented level of civil society participation in the facility. Over thirty programs operated by nonstate entities are present inside Angola, including a fully accredited theology curriculum offered by the New Orleans Baptist Theological Seminary. Another aspect of Angola's uniqueness is that over 70 percent of the inmates are serving life sentences and over 90 percent will die inside Angola (Hallett et al. 2015). Despite the comparatively rich offerings for personal and spiritual growth, it is still a very heavy place.

My interest in religious practice inside prison was the impetus for the tour, so when we arrived at the seminary building, I asked my guide if I could speak with a seminary student. The guide spoke to another guard who nodded his head in approval. I heard my guide ask, "Which one should we have him talk to?" The guard responded without the slightest hesitation: "Charlie. Let's have him talk with Charlie." In less than five minutes, an inmate dressed in prison-issue blue jeans, a white T-shirt, and a frayed gray overcoat emerged from the bunkhouse. After a short introduction, I asked a few basic questions about the seminary classes and his thoughts on the program.

Charlie gave a glowing review of the curriculum, but as we spoke, he made repeated eye contact with the guard, who stood two feet behind me listening to our conversation. I didn't doubt the sincerity of Charlie's response, but as we continued to talk, it was clear that the presence of the prison guard had a direct influence on the conversation—I knew I was getting a sanitized version of Charlie's experience. But what did I expect? I was there for one afternoon and standing next to a guard.

After ten minutes, I thanked Charlie for his time and finished the tour by visiting the hound-dog pen, execution chamber, and the nine-hole golf course maintained by the inmates. Angola is an interesting place, but the experience convinced me that to collect reliable data I would need to participate in something beyond a prison tour.

APAC—WHERE THE INMATES RUN THE PRISON

I took the lessons I learned in Angola and applied them to the Brazilian context. I wanted a situation where I could experience prison life with limited interference from the administration and maximize the amount of "back-stage" interactions with the inmates. Through preliminary research for the project and connections from previous work in Brazil, I located a prison system in the state of Minas Gerais that used a distinctive penology. APAC (Associação de Proteção e Assistência aos Condenados, or the Association for Protection and Assistance of Convicts) is a prison system that implements a unique restorative penal theory that is now operating in almost thirty cities in Minas Gerais, a state with a population of about twenty million.

Dr. Mario Ottoboni, a lawyer and passionate Catholic, founded APAC in 1972. Ottoboni faced a crisis in his personal faith after seeing the conditions of the prison in his hometown. Horrified by what he saw, he set out to create an experimental prison system based on a unique application of the golden rule: *Treat imprisoned people the way you would want them to treat others* (Ottoboni 2003, 24). Ottoboni's penology was based on the simple premise that if the prisoner is treated with dignity and respect, the prisons will run better and offer an environment that is conducive to personal transformation. He believed prisons could be places of restoration and not simply punishment.

One of the defining aspects of the APAC methodology is the absence of prison guards. Opponents have criticized the practice as absurd and dangerous to the local community because these facilities hold men and women convicted of murder, rape, and armed assaults. Because the inmates at the APAC facilities would still be locked in cells at night to fulfill government requirements, Ottoboni argued that they should be trusted to hold the keys to the cells and hold each other accountable to APAC's rehabilitative goals. Though the strategy is definitely nontraditional, taking armed guards out of the prison effectively eliminates the tension that usually exists between guards and inmates (while prison riots are common in Brazil, there has never been a riot in the APAC system) and changes the culture of the prison. More importantly, the absence of prison guards sends a clear message to the inmates that they are worthy of trust and that the expectations for them are not only to serve sentences, but also to leave the prison as better citizens.

In most cases, the APAC prisons operate parallel to the traditional prison system and hold between 50 to 75 percent of a given city's inmate population. Inmates are initially placed in the state-run jail and after about six months are allowed to voluntarily transfer to an APAC prison. Living conditions in the APAC prisons are considerably better than in the "normal" prisons, so while there are no guards watching over the inmates, the threat of being sent back to the state-run jail serves as an effective deterrent to breaking the rules. Though the cells at the APAC prison are full of violent offenders, the recruitment process and enrollment criteria ensure that inmates judged as active threats to themselves or others are not allowed into the APAC prisons.

APAC staff see their system as a revolutionary model of imprisonment, and they actively try to export their vision and innovative penology to other parts of Brazil, as well as neighboring countries in South America and parts of Africa. One of the reasons that my request to stay in the prison as an inmate was granted is because APAC's leadership was confident that their prisons truly were safe places, even though they housed inmates convicted of violent crimes. Another reason I was granted access was that, assuming I made it out of the prison without issue, having a foreigner spend time in a Brazilian prison and live to tell a positive tale would serve as further evidence of the prison's safety and the success of the APAC system.

THE FIRST WEEK

In my cell that first day, I finished unpacking about an hour before the evening meal. Most of the inmates were either playing soccer in the concrete patio or smoking cigarettes while huddled around a twelve-inch television set at the end of the cellblock. Unsure of what to do, I gingerly made my way out of my cell and shuffled aimlessly down the hallway. Immediately, a wiry man in his early thirties, wearing a tight afro and seldom blinking, emerged from his cell and greeted me with a firm handshake. He smiled broadly, introduced himself as the "president" of the cellblock, and, reading the concern written on my face, repeatedly emphasized that I shouldn't be worried: "You will be safe," he said.

I knew I had a lot to learn about prison life. Though the APAC system was substantially safer than other prisons in Brazil, it was nonetheless a very different social world than either the neighborhood in suburban Minneapolis where I grew up or the university campus where I had hatched my research plan.

My goal was to fit into the prison population as best I could. Intent on dressing in a way that matched the inmate fashion aesthetic, I had bought a pair of generic sweatpants and a gray sweatshirt at a discount clothing stand close to the prison, guessing the other inmates would be wearing something similar. APAC inmates do not wear prison uniforms (another component of the APAC methodology), and my guess was accurate—a number of the men had the same type of outfit. My choice to show up with a thick beard, however, was not nearly as astute.

I didn't realize that beards were not allowed in the APAC prison, and in my desire to "fit in," I was determined to shave. Unfortunately, the one disposable razor I had brought with me was not up to the challenge. My cellmate walked in during my unsuccessful attempt at shaving, and I introduced myself to him while dabbing at the blood trickling down my chin with a towel. He laughed and made a joke about how I needed a prison razor, or a "tractor" as he called it. In less than a minute he had ripped the blade guard off my disposable razor and melted away the excess plastic with his cigarette lighter. The customized instrument he handed back to me would have shaved the fur off a grizzly bear, but the slightest slip could mean stitches. The beard was gone in a few minutes.

As I shaved and chatted with my cellmate, I discovered the administration had failed to tell the inmates in my wing about me. I explained to my cellmate why I would be rooming with him for the week. By the time dinner was served, word about who I was and why I was there had spread among the eighty men living in the prison. My initial interaction with my cellmate—his help with the razor—foreshadowed the way I would be treated by the other men in the cellblock throughout the week. The three men in my cell and a dozen other inmates I gravitated toward consistently looked out for me. They made sure I learned the unwritten rules of the prison and gave me cues on how to conduct myself during the days and nights.

They also welcomed me into their space with small gestures, like loaning me a cup to carry in my pocket for the morning coffee and water at every meal. During my first meal, I accepted a sample of pepper sauce an inmate made in his cell. I thanked him and told him that I liked it. For the rest of the week he found me at mealtime and gave me a couple of spoonfuls to help enliven the bland food. In general, the men in my cellblock graciously accepted me into their world for the week and were more than generous with their hospitality. As one inmate told me, "You are our guest. We get a lot of visitors, but nobody has come to live with us."

There were three other men in my cell. The inmate on the bunk below mine was serving time for smuggling cocaine in from Paraguay, and he snored louder than anyone I have ever met. The guy who modified my razor had been incarcerated for over a year and was serving a sentence for a series of armed robberies he had committed to feed an ugly crack habit. The third person in the cell was accused of a sexual crime, the details of which I never asked, nor were they offered. The sex offender spent nearly all of his waking hours sitting on his bed chain-smoking while listening to news on a portable radio. He had very little contact with anyone else in the prison. I decided before I arrived that I wouldn't ask anyone about his criminal convictions or why he was in prison. But by the end of the week I knew why nearly all of the men were confined in the cellblock. The crimes ranged from murder to armed assault and drug dealing. Though some of the inmates told me their sentence was too harsh, nobody said he was innocent.

DAILY SCHEDULE

Days in the prison had a slow, deliberate rhythm and quickly became predictable. The breakfast line started to form at 7:20 A.M., and food was served ten minutes later. There wasn't a bell, but nobody overslept, and the morning ritual of reciting the Lord's Prayer didn't start until everyone was present. The breakfast menu never changed, and the small cup of sickly sweet coffee and a piece of buttered bread were consumed in solemn silence. A palpable gloom hung in the air each morning. It is depressing to wake up in prison.

The inmates at APAC are required to "work" throughout the day. Time was taken off their sentences for each day they worked, but in the highest security section of the facility where I stayed, the work options were limited. Most of the men filled their time making handicrafts with donated scraps of wood or cloth. During the morning and afternoon, the prison looked a little like a middle-school art class as the men made welcome mats, picture frames, wooden toys, plaques honoring professional soccer teams, and other trinkets. A few of the finished products were for sale in the lobby, but most of them were passed to family members on visiting day.

The men formed small groups as they worked on their projects and chatted with each other throughout the day. I spent the week making a wooden wall hanging under the tutelage of a few of the inmates, and I tried to join a different group each day while I worked in order to talk to as many of the men as possible. The first foreigner that many of the inmates had ever spoken with, I had no trouble joining in the conversations. In fact, I spent a lot of my time answering questions about the United States. What did I think of President Obama? Why does the United States use the death penalty? What is the street value of cocaine where I live? Did Keith Richards really snort a line of his father's cremated ashes?

I answered every question as best I could, but eventually many of the conversations turned to the inmates' court cases. While the men were officially discouraged from talking about their specific crimes, I heard dozens of detailed stories about international drug-smuggling operations, successful and botched assaults on banks and buses, as well as the nuances of the small-time cocaine and marijuana trade on the streets just outside the prison. Most of the men who were serving time for murder didn't talk about their cases, and those convicted of sexual crimes completely avoided participating in these conversations.

BUILDING TRUST THROUGH SOCCER

Between the afternoon work shift and supper, there were ninety minutes of "free time." Some men rested, others watched the news, but most of the younger inmates played in the daily soccer game in a seventy- by forty-foot enclosed concrete patio that had a small (and, from my perspective, very dangerous) wall jutting out from one side. The games were intense, rough, and peppered with shouted empty threats. Many of the inmates played barefoot. After watching the first five minutes of play, I decided that I would remain a spectator and take no part in this slice of prison life. I enjoy sports, but the game was rough, and I had a real fear of having my nose broken by one of the shots blasted in the tight quarters or crashing head first into the concrete wall. I was thoroughly intimidated.

Four-man teams played the games, and the first team that scored two goals won the match. Once the second goal was scored, four new players arrived on the court as the winners celebrated and taunted the losing team as they made their exit. I stood along the wall, comfortable as an observer, but to my dismay, when one game finished, the inmate in charge of choosing the next team pointed at me and told me that I was on his team. My first instinct was to smile, joke about how Americans are terrible soccer players, and follow through on the decision that I had already made not to play. But as I started to refuse the invitation, I realized that this is exactly what I had signed up for, so I decided to go to my cell, change into shorts, and grab my shoes.

It took me a few games to get accustomed to the pace of play. The first day, I was left out of the pushing, grabbing, and hard tackles. With my limited soccer skills, I played tentatively and as inconspicuously as possible, but I started to feel more comfortable and confident as the day progressed. In a game toward the end of the second day, I ran to control a ball in the corner. An opposing player pushed me in the small of my back with his forearm. My shoulder hit the wall, I fell off balance, and he easily kicked the ball away from me. I responded angrily with an instinctual shove to my opponent's shoulder blade and received nothing but a mocking laugh in return. The shoves we exchanged proved to be an important turning point when I realized that it was a sign of acceptance more than anything malicious.

The games were one of the few times during the day when inmates seemed to briefly forget where they were. As for me, the physical exertion provided a release from the monotony of confinement and gave me an invaluable opportunity to interact with the other inmates as a teammate or opponent, not as a social science researcher. During the heat of competition, it didn't matter that I was a foreign sociologist and my teammates were convicted murderers, low-level drug dealers, or bank robbers; I could push them and they could push me. I loosened up, increased my intensity, and enjoyed the competition.

As a result, I had the chance to genuinely participate in post-goal celebrations and to absorb the fleeting wrath of teammates I had let down with a poor play that led to an opponent's goal. When I scored my first goal after three afternoons, I pretended it wasn't a big deal, but as my teammates circled around and patted me on the back, laughing that the gringo finally scored, I couldn't help but grin from ear to ear.

I played with the same guys each afternoon, and we developed friendships that carried over to the rest of the day and throughout the week. I joined in the banter in the dining hall about the feats and failures in the games, and I was even part of a group that was scolded by the inmate president for playing too late and not showing up for dinner on time. My participation in the games bought me a bit of credibility and, more importantly, provided a way to build relationships quickly.

SHAPING A METHODOLOGY

I had read about the "pains of imprisonment" in Gresham Sykes's (1958) enduringly influential book *The Society of Captives*, but seeing how these pains manifested in the lives of people I knew personally helped me to understand them in a different, more tangible way. One of the "pains" Sykes describes is that of an inmate cut off from his or her family and loved ones. I saw how the prison lit up on Sunday afternoon during the weekly family visiting time. Preparations began on Saturday night as the inmates gave each other haircuts. There was one trimmer and one incarcerated barber, so we waited in line and by the time the families arrived on Sunday afternoon, everyone, even those who knew nobody was coming to visit him, was showered, shaved, and dressed in his best clothes.

Upon arrival, passionate kisses were exchanged between the men and their wives or girlfriends. I saw mothers of teenage inmates pull their boys close and warmly stroke their faces. I choked up when I saw three- and four-year-old children sprint to their fathers and cling to legs, tugging their shirts asking to be picked up and held. Young kids screamed and laughed as they chased one another between the chairs and under the tables, oblivious to the fact that they were in a prison. They were just happy to see their dads.

At four in the afternoon, the visitors had to leave and as they let go of their last hugs, I heard the same line delivered from a number of mothers to their confused toddlers: "No, my child, Daddy can't come with us; he has to stay here for just a little while longer." When the families left they took with them all of the temporary joy that their visit had brought. The hours immediately following the Sunday visit were the most depressing of the week, and the heavy sorrow that settled in the cellblock would not disappear until Monday morning.

I wasn't a real prisoner during this part of the fieldwork. I hadn't been convicted of a crime and I knew that I could leave if I wanted to. I hope I never really "know" what it actually feels like to be imprisoned, but the time I spent behind bars at least gave me a taste. I vividly remember lying wide-awake on the top bunk in my cell one Thursday night when I couldn't sleep and my cellmate in the bunk below had been snoring nonstop for over three hours. I had never heard anyone snore so loudly for so long. The entire bunk shook.

Lying on my back, I looked over my toes and through the bars of the window to see the moon shining brightly in the deep black sky and I started thinking, "What if I had to spend ten years in this place?" Maybe we have all asked ourselves, "What if I were in prison?" I know that I have. Lying in the prison cell that evening, the question was no longer an abstract exercise because I was asking myself, "Could I handle ten years sleeping in *this* bed behind *these* bars?" I was overcome with despair just thinking about the hypothetical situation. I had spent four days in the prison, and ten years seemed like an eternity; I didn't know whether or how I could do it. I kept thinking about what a tragic waste it would be for my life and what incredible pain it would cause my family. Those emotions, mixed with regret or remorse over the crime I may have committed or the pain that my action had caused others, would be a torturous combination. I cannot pretend to understand how individuals cope with such thoughts, but when I woke the next morning I understood why there were no smiles in the breakfast line.

JAILHOUSE RELIGION

My first experience with organized religion inside prison came on the third night of my stay, a Wednesday. I had finished dinner and gone back to my cell to grab a sweatshirt before joining the nightly, never-ending domino game. On my way there, one of the inmates tapped my shoulder and told me, "Hey, the church is coming."

Most evenings I spent in the prison were the same. One group of men played dominos, another watched melodramatic Brazilian soap operas, some of the younger inmates sat around strumming a guitar, and one inmate paced continuously from wall to wall, counting aloud hundreds of laps. To be honest, I was ready for a change of pace and the service offered a break in the routine. We walked toward a side room where three volunteers from a local Assembly of God congregation stood dressed in blue jeans and T-shirts and armed with Bibles and an acoustic guitar. They shook hands and greeted a few regular attendees, unpacked the guitar, and almost immediately started to sing worship choruses familiar to everyone in the room.

An inmate who had been convicted of a drug-related murder came to the service late and sat in the empty chair to my left. I had kept my distance from him because he was a bit of a loner who maintained a "tough guy" façade and started fights during the soccer games. When I sat close to him during the afternoon work hours, I overheard him bragging callously about the homicide he had committed. He was the only inmate who called me "gringo" to my face and went out of his way to give me a hard time, so I wasn't thrilled when he chose the open chair next to me. As the volunteers played the songs, all of the inmates stood up and sang along, but the young man on my left remained in his chair, detached and defiant.

Once the music started, passion and emotion filled the room. A number of the men wiped tears from their eyes as they sang with their arms stretched to the ceiling, eyes squeezed shut, reaching out to an unseen God. During the chorus of the third or fourth song, I glanced at the man to my left. He was still sitting, but now his head hung low with his hands folded between his knees. His shoulders shook as he gently sobbed and I could see tears form tiny puddles on his heavily tattooed arms.

After the singing, one of the Pentecostal volunteers gave a fifteen-minute sermon on a New Testament passage. There was no idle chatter during any part of the service, and after the closing prayer, the volunteers thanked the men for coming and offered to pray individually for anyone who asked. The inmates started to form two- and three-person lines, waiting for their chance to stand face-to-face with one of the volunteers. When an inmate finished sharing his requests, the volunteer placed his hand on his head or shoulder and prayed aloud for the man's family, upcoming parole decisions, or simply for strength to make it through the next week. In an act that I would see repeated frequently during my fieldwork, once the prayer was finished the volunteer would tightly embrace the prisoner in a full five-second hug. Outside of the family visit and the soccer games' high-fives, the post-prayer hug was the only display of physical affection between people I witnessed during the week.

When I arrived at the prison, I hadn't narrowed my research focus to anything more specific than "religion inside prisons in Brazil." As the week progressed, it was clear to me that Pentecostalism resonated with these men in a unique way. I decided to narrow my study and focus solely on Pentecostalism inside prison for three reasons. First, the emotionally charged worship service resonated with the inmates more profoundly than I had expected and I was moved by the urgency in the inmates' voices as they sang and cried out in song. Second, only a few of the dozens of inmates I interviewed reported being practicing Catholics. Even though the prison was in a predominantly Catholic region of Brazil, the vast majority of the interviewees spoke about converting or returning to a heavily Pentecostal version of Protestantism. Finally, the number of Pentecostal volunteers, pastors, and teachers who visited the prison outnumbered volunteers from any other religious affiliation by more than ten to one. This ratio was disproportionate to the surrounding community, where Pentecostals were the minority.

Three weeks after I left the first APAC prison, I spent another week in a different APAC facility about one hundred miles away. Though the second prison was also in a predominantly Catholic community, I saw quite clearly that Pentecostalism was the dominant faith behind bars there as well. By the time I had finished spending two weeks inside of these prisons, I had refined my research topic from "religion in Brazilian prisons" to "Pentecostalism in Brazilian prisons."

RIO DE JANEIRO: BEAUTIFUL BEACHES AND MEDIEVAL DUNGEONS

Even though I started the research in the APAC prisons in the state of Minas Gerais, I knew that I was going to situate the bulk of the fieldwork in Rio de Janeiro. My time in the APAC prison system provided me with firsthand experience of prison life and a glimpse of the emotions, daily routines, and subcultural norms behind bars. Though the prisons in Rio de Janeiro were very different places from those I visited in Minas Gerais, the two weeks I spent "as an inmate" served as a foundation for the rest of my methodology.

But the time I spent living in the cells did not prepare me for what I encountered in Rio, where the jails and prisons made the APAC prisons in Minas Gerais seem like members-only country clubs. Salgado Jail, one of my primary research sites in Rio de Janeiro, was located on the corner of a busy street in a tough and gritty impoverished suburb on the outskirts of the city.[1] Inmates were brought here immediately after their arrest and remained in the cellblocks until their trial. Some waited more than two years to see a judge. During my fieldwork nearly half of the over five thousand people incarcerated in Rio de Janeiro were held in jails like Salgado.[2] Since the space in the city's penitentiaries was highly regulated and the number of inmates did not exceed the number of beds, the jails became holding tanks and were nearly bursting at the seams with inmates awaiting trial.

Much of Salgado's concrete exterior had been chipped away and the exposed patches of dull gray cement added to the neighborhood's general state of disrepair. This part of the city is a long way, both geographically and culturally, from the iconic beach neighborhoods of Copacabana and Ipanema. There could be up to eight hundred inmates inside the detention center at any given time, and on weekday mornings, hundreds of people lined up and waited to spend an hour with their son, brother, husband, boyfriend, or father.

The visitor's line was not a joyful place, and nine out of ten people waiting to enter the jail were either women or children. Every time I visited, I saw mothers and grandmothers with tired, defeated expressions standing in line, holding plastic containers of rice and beans. I heard them scold their children and grandchildren when they got agitated, reminding them that they had to be on their best behavior because they were going to visit Daddy "at work." The white lie served its purpose at the moment, but it would not be long before the children understood.

Teenage girls stood in the same line but were less somber, often frantically applying the last touches of lipstick or eyeliner before seeing their incarcerated boyfriends. These young girls, like everyone else in the visiting line, had to pay 10 Reais (at the time about $4) to enter the facility and another 10 Reais if they wanted to bring in a container of food. I overheard one woman say that she was happy her boyfriend was transferred to Salgado because it was cheaper to visit than the last jail. The jail's "cover charge" was illegal, so the cash was discreetly handed from the visitor to the inmate during the visit. After the visit ended, the inmate put the money into a guard's hands on the way back to the cellblock. The money collected was divided and distributed among the guards later in the afternoon.

When a visitor approached the entrance to the jail, a small sheet-metal door swung open into the jail's makeshift waiting room. Family members, pastors, and the occasional lawyer had to approach a desk, sign their names in a book, show identification, and present any food they brought for inspection. Then they passed through the gray, cracked-plastic metal detector adjacent to the sign-in desk. I saw hundreds of people pass through the metal detector, but after a few months of total silence from the machine, I started to question whether it was actually plugged in and functioning. Not everything in Salgado was up to code.

Past the metal detector, the building opened into a small dirt courtyard where a half-dozen "trustees" spent the day on folding chairs, talking soccer, reading the newspaper, or admiring the most recent Brazilian edition of *Playboy*. Officially, these men were inmates, but they were also members of a growing mafia in Rio that has strong connections to the police department. Because of their mafia affiliation, these men lived in a separate section of the jail (called the VIP room by the inmates) and they served as the de facto security detail, taking orders from the police officers who were officially in charge. The mafia-affiliated inmates held the keys to the cells and supervised the visiting hours. They were the ones who entered the cellblocks to remove an inmate. The guards and police officers knew better than to go behind the iron bars and into the cellblocks.

The jail itself was not particularly remarkable on the outside or in the entrance area, but the interior was unforgettable. The cellblock area was divided into two units—essentially a pair of dungeons. Each unit comprised five cells originally built to house fifteen to eighteen inmates. The building's architects would have been shocked if they could have seen the cells they had designed regularly stuffed with fifty or sixty detainees—up to eighty on the worst days. In the evening the men would sleep head-to-toe on the concrete slabs that served as beds. Other inmates slept shoulder-to-shoulder on the floor, and those without a spot to sleep either waited upright until something opened up or tied their chests to the bars with t-shirts and slept standing.

The conditions inside the cells are hard to describe, but nearly everyone I met who had seen them used the word "dungeon" at some point to describe Salgado's cells. The concrete walls in the cells were painted white years ago, but during the fieldwork, they were streaked black with layers of dirt, dried sweat, and mildew. Large sections of the walls were wallpapered in pornography, and the seductive smiles of hundreds of nude women staring out from the faded magazine photos created a bizarre juxtaposition between lust and misery.

Each cell had a bathroom with an eight-inch hole in the ground that served as the toilet and a cold-water spigot eight feet above for the shower. The line to use it was continuous but orderly. Unwritten rules enforced by the inmates dictated nearly every action—from where a person sleeps to when they could use the bathroom. There were no windows, so ventilation was nearly nonexistent, and the only light came from small television sets hung from the cell bars with bedsheets that had been twisted into ropes. Six months before I arrived, a volunteer from Rio de Paz, a local nongovernmental organization (NGO), made the newspaper front pages by posing in one of the cells with a thermometer in his hands that read 56.7° C (134° F).[3]

The dank, rotting smell that filled the cellblocks was only thinly masked by cheap industrial disinfectant and cigarette smoke. The air inside was heavy, wet, and hard to inhale. But the heat and the smell were not the most jarring aspects of Salgado's cellblocks; the quantity of human beings crammed into each cell won that prize. When the cell doors were locked, shirtless inmates had to squeeze shoulder-to-shoulder for all the bodies to fit in the cell.

The only provision offered by the state was the three meals served each day. The food, often rancid, was delivered to the cells in a foam cooler and the inmates dispersed it among themselves. Inmates fortunate enough to have a regular visitor willing to deliver food and pay the cover charge could avoid the official fare. The jail's guards sold meals made in their kitchen to inmates willing to pay, but those without a visitor or money to buy the guards' food were left with no other options.

Not surprisingly, the inmates in Salgado were not healthy. Besides the poor nutrition, many of the men arrived with open wounds and deep purple bruises acquired from the police during their arrest. The ill and most severely wounded inmates were allowed to lie on the floor next to the steel bars to get the best chance at fresh air. Other prisoners, shot during their capture, were simply thrown into the cells. Since there was no medical care at Salgado, an inmate who'd worked at a hospital years before had assumed the duty of jailhouse doctor. On a shelf, he proudly displayed a dozen flattened bullets and pieces of shrapnel that he had pulled from the flesh of arriving inmates.

Despite these dismal conditions, a bit of humor and irony survived in Salgado. The part of the prison that held the mafia members and other inmates who paid hefty bribes to the guards was called the VIP section. It was separate from the other cellblock units and offered, for a steep price, a significantly better prison experience. The VIP section had air-conditioning, beds with mattresses, a working refrigerator, a television, a DVD player, and a full kitchen. On my visits to this area, I was offered cold soda, bread, cheese, fruit, coffee, and the best fried chicken I have ever tasted, prepared by the inmates in the VIP section. This part of Salgado was a far cry from the conditions experienced by the other inmates in cells fewer than twenty yards away. But like the velvet-roped VIP lounges of chic nightclubs, the VIP area in Salgado was not open to just anyone. To stay in this area, an inmate had to have the right connections and he had to pay, and pay dearly. There was no set price; it fluctuated depending on the inmates' connections and suspected wealth, but I heard rumors that it would be cheaper to rent an apartment overlooking the beach at Copacabana than to reserve a good spot in the VIP section at Salgado.

Rio de Janeiro's prisons were more orderly, monitored more closely, and also more difficult to gain access to than the jails. I visited four of the city's jails, which held arrestees before trials, and two prisons that housed the convicted, but I focused my research in Salgado and one prison, Cinza Penitentiary. Cinza, scheduled for demolition before the opening ceremony of the 2016 Olympic Games, was a large dilapidated building that looked like an airplane hangar. It was essentially a long corridor lined with more than a dozen cells, each equipped with fifty beds. The cells at Cinza were not nearly as crowded as Salgado, and each man had his own bed. I was not able to gain the same sort of access that I did in Salgado, but many of the sights, smells, and sounds were similar to those in the jails.

Unlike Salgado, the men incarcerated at Cinza had already been convicted and were serving their sentences. This changed the environment inside the cellblocks. Cinza's inmates didn't hope for a generous judge or a witness's changed testimony. They had received their sentences and were doing their time. One of the differences between the prison system in Brazil and the United States is the length of the sentences. Sentences are significantly shorter in Brazil and life without parole does not exist. Coming from the United States, I was surprised to hear that inmates serving time for murder would likely be out of prison and in a halfway house within five to seven years, sometimes sooner.

While I asked a police officer about differences in the sentencing requirements between the United States and Brazil, he asked me if

I had read the Brazilian constitution. I knew I was being set up for a punch line, but I dutifully responded that I had not. He responded, "Well, every Brazilian citizen has the right to kill one person. Once you kill a second person, then we will really punish you." Though the officer was making a joke, the sentences for Brazilian inmates are drastically shorter than those doled out by the US system for similar crimes. Unlike places like Angola in Louisiana, which is a terminal destination for nearly all of the inmates, very few of the Brazilian prisoners will be incarcerated for more than ten years.

GAINING ACCESS

I visited Salgado two or three times a week for nearly a year in order to observe worship services and to conduct interviews with the inmates. I was not able to gain the same sort of access to Cinza, but I visited there monthly over a six-month period. My access to these places was unique—especially in Salgado, where I was able to spend hundreds of hours and conducted dozens of interviews because of the relationships I developed with the prison administration, the pastors and other volunteers who visited the prisons and jails regularly, and the inmates themselves.

The warden at Salgado was the key to the success of my methodology. When I met him, I presented my research plan and told him how I wanted to implement it in his jail. The warden was skeptical about religious practice inside prison, but over time we developed a rapport, and he eventually agreed to the proposal and told his staff that I could enter the facility when I pleased.

Even though I had the warden's permission and I eventually became a fixture inside the jail, I never had full support from the guards in Salgado. There was real animosity between the inmates and the police officers guarding the jail. A battle between the police and the narco-gangs has been raging for nearly thirty years in Rio de Janeiro, resulting in the deaths of thousands of gang members and police officers. In some ways Salgado was a prisoner-of-war camp. I believe I was never fully trusted by the police officers because they thought my allegiance was with the inmates—or, in their eyes, the enemy. Occasionally the officers greeted me with open hostility when I arrived, and sometimes without explanation I was not allowed to enter the jail. More than once I was sent away with colorful and creative cursing.

For reasons never made clear, one of the officers always refused to let me into the jail when he was guarding the door. It didn't seem to matter what I said; he always sent me away and appeared to take pleasure in watching me shuffle back dejectedly to my bus stop for the two-hour journey back to my apartment. If traffic was bad I could count on a six-hour round trip.

I came to dread the moment when I got off the bus and approached the metal garage door that served as the only entrance to the jail. Some mornings I had to take a series of deep breaths to work up the courage just to knock on the door. Other days, the entire facility was on lockdown as punishment for an inmate infraction or as retribution for an uptick of crime in the streets. During lockdown, all families and visitors were sent away, many with return trips much longer and costlier than mine.

I was marginally successful in mitigating some of the hostility by engaging the police officers in conversation during the day and by eating lunch with them. I also interviewed a few of the officers in an attempt not only to get their perspective on the jail, but also to let them know that I was interested in their thoughts and not just what the inmates had to say. Still, I understood the officers' reaction to my presence in the jail. Because I spent so much unmonitored time inside the cellblocks, I could be transferring information to parties outside the prison or used in a number of other ways by the inmates. Another reason was that Salgado Jail was saturated with corruption. From the cover fee charged to visitors, to the rent collected in the VIP section, to the drugs that consistently found their way into the cells and the inmates that mysteriously disappeared, there were numerous activities the police did not want advertised. In their eyes, the "benefit" of an ethnographic study of religion inside prison did not outweigh the risks of the wrong sort of information getting out.

I first entered Salgado with Rio de Paz, an NGO led by the Presbyterian pastor Antonio Carlos Costa and composed primarily of volunteers from his church. Every other Saturday, the group would visit Salgado and bring in a portable medical station with trained medical professionals to do everything from pulling teeth to treating infected wounds. Each time the volunteers from Rio de Paz visited Salgado they held two worship services: one for anyone living in the five cells "owned" by Rio's largest gang (the Comando Vermelho [CV]), and a separate service for the inmates in the other wing. I benefited tremendously from my association with Rio de Paz because of the goodwill they had built among the inmate population and the initial access and credibility they provided me.

Toward the end of my first visit to Salgado, I asked if I could introduce myself to the leaders of the prison church. In just a few minutes, three men were led out of the cells in handcuffs and brought to the visiting room to speak with me. The men sat across from me dressed in plain white T-shirts, knee-length shorts, and flip-flop sandals. They squinted as their eyes adjusted to the strong fluorescent lights, then asked who I was. I introduced myself, explained why I was there, and started in with a few questions. The inmates were standoffish at first—more intent on figuring out this gringo sitting in front of them than on answering questions. Pedro identified himself as the pastor, and Eder and Jobson told me that they were *obreros*, or workers in the church.[4]

Pedro was silent and looked at me with an intense stare. I looked down at my feet to break the eye contact, but he never flinched. The skin on his broad face hung loosely over his cheekbones as if he had recently lost weight, and his large hands, strengthened by years of construction work, wrapped around a weathered leather Bible. Suddenly nervous and intimidated, I struggled to find the right Portuguese words to say. Pastor Pedro interrupted me in midsentence and transitioned from interviewee to interviewer.

He started in with his own set of questions, and I was able to regain my composure as I spoke about the time I had spent in Minas Gerais and my vision for the research. I stressed that my interest was to learn about how religion was practiced among the inmates in the jail and how the church operated within these spaces. Our meeting only lasted twenty minutes, but at the end of our time together the church leaders understood my intentions and were enthusiastic about speaking to me about their church. They were clearly proud of the church that they had built inside the cellblocks. The Rio de Paz team was about to leave, so we concluded our meeting and each of the three men gave me a quick hug and told me they would be happy to participate in the research.

After the first visit with Rio de Paz, I started spending more time around the jail trying to learn more about it and find a way to visit the inmates more frequently than every two weeks with the NGO. Every morning just before ten o'clock, and sometimes again in the afternoon, small groups of Pentecostals from local congregations arrived at the jail's entrance to lead a worship service in the cells. Besides the volunteers from Rio de Paz, these groups were the only members of civil society I saw enter the jail. Some of the groups brought a portable sound system and a guitar, while others arrived with nothing more than a Bible and a tambourine tucked under their arms. Most of the volunteers were members of humble, storefront Pentecostal churches located within a few miles of the prison.

Twelve groups of Pentecostal volunteers visited the prison each week. In theory, each group would arrive on a specific day and hold a service with the inmates, but nothing was written down on paper. After a series of "double bookings," in which two groups showed up at the same time, the prison administration called a meeting to write up a new schedule and assign each group a time slot.

Representatives from all of the involved Pentecostal churches arrived at the jail for this meeting, and after clearing it with the warden, I introduced myself to the group, explained my project, and asked if I could accompany them into the cells during their services. Each of the groups agreed to my request and, the next day, I joined the Pentecostal teams when they held their worship services in the cellblocks. This arrangement allowed me to build rapport with the inmates at Salgado because I was able to see the men multiple times per week. It also allowed me, throughout the year of fieldwork, to develop relationships with the churches that were located in the surrounding neighborhoods.

After months of consistent contact with the inmates in the jail, I began to occupy a unique place in Salgado Jail, specifically with members of the inmate church. A few of the men I knew well had me call their families to tell them if the visiting schedule had been abruptly changed. Dozens of the men in the jail hadn't been able to communicate with their families since their arrest, and some of them had gone months without any outside contact. Nearly every week I was asked to make a phone call to the family of a new arrival to Salgado to tell them their son was alive, but in jail. Some of these calls were awkward given the circumstances, but my willingness to play this role brought me tremendous favor and gratitude from the inmates, and it allowed me to talk with a few of the families of Salgado's inmates. As I spent more time in the jail I was invited to lunch or coffee at the homes of a number of the inmates' families, and I attended services at some of their home churches.

With the reluctant blessing of the jail's warden I started recording interviews the following Monday and amassed fifteen interviews during the first six weeks. I was given access to a small room not much larger than a walk-in closet that served as my office during the day. At night, the guards rented out the space as an ad hoc conjugal visit room. A bribe paid to the on-duty police officer bought an inmate time in the room and safe passage from the street for a wife, girlfriend, or prostitute. I used the "multipurpose" room to record interviews with the detainees who participated in the prison church and with anyone else willing to talk to me. It was an excellent space because I could shut the door and talk to the men in privacy. The guards knew who was in the room at all times and occasionally interrupted by barging in unannounced, but they never censored any of my questions or observed the interviews. I recorded a total of twenty interviews inside Salgado, but after a wave of gang violence on the streets of Rio de Janeiro, I was no longer allowed to bring a recorder into the jail.

Recruiting inmates to participate was not a problem. I offered glasses of cold water and promised not to ask any questions about their criminal charges. Being interviewed meant an hour or so out of the cells, so many of the men jumped at the opportunity. When Nestor, the inmate church's worship leader, arrived, he told me, "Thanks for calling me; what a blessing from God. This is the first time I have seen the sun in three months." After the interview was finished, I opened the door to my "office" and called the trustee to lead him back to the cells. Nestor was escorted across the open-air courtyard in handcuffs and just before he arrived at the hallway leading to his cell, he stopped and looked up at the sky, squinting to steal one more glimpse of the sun.

HOSPITALITY AND THE INMATES' CODE

The methodology I used raised some eyebrows when I explained it to people living in Rio de Janeiro. Questions about my safety were the most frequent responses to my story. They were certainly fair questions, given the reputation of Rio's prisons and the fact that, while some of the inmates had been arrested for nonviolent crimes like drug distribution or shoplifting, most were incarcerated for armed assault or a violent attack.

There were times when I was worried, and there could have been times when my personal safety may have been at risk. But based on the hundreds of hours I spent in the cellblocks in the APAC prisons as well as the jails and prisons in Rio de Janeiro, I can honestly report that the inmates I encountered could not have treated me with more respect and hospitality. There was a separate set of rules inside prison that was strictly followed by the inmates and just as strictly enforced by the inmate leaders, especially the gang leaders. Treating visitors with respect was one of these rules, and there was significant pressure to obey. I was never overtly intimidated or hassled by the men in prison and I was never asked to do anything illegal.

The first time I visited the gang-controlled section of Salgado, the gang leader—called "the president"—called for the attention of the entire wing as I was about to leave, and within thirty seconds the radios and televisions were turned off and all conversations stopped. Even the buzz from the electric tattoo needle being used on the bicep of an inmate in the corner stopped. In the silence that followed, the gang leader spoke to me and said, "I want to thank you for coming in here today. People on the outside think we are a bunch of caged animals in here, but as you can see we are not. I want you to know that you are welcome here anytime." As I left, I shook hands with at least two dozen gang members. I had not expected to be received so warmly by the Comando Vermelho.

At first, I admit that I was shocked at the reverence I witnessed from the inmates toward myself and the other visitors (which were almost exclusively Pentecostal volunteers) in Salgado, but as I continued the fieldwork, I encountered this sort of treatment in every facility I entered. I don't know everything that went on behind those bars when I was not there, and it is possible, though unlikely, that the inmates were simply putting on a show for the outsiders, but I can only report on my experience. After just a few weeks, I was no longer hesitant to go into the cellblocks at Salgado even though I knew that there would be no guards or police officers to protect me if something went awry. I developed a deep trust in this aspect of the inmate code and could not have completed the research without the hospitality and respect that were shown to me by the incarcerated men I met during this project.

CHAPTER 2

THE KILLABLE PEOPLE

The Comando Vermelho's fire-bombing campaign brought life in Rio de Janeiro to a screeching halt during the last week of November 2010. Gang members torched dozens of vehicles in response to the police and military invasion and occupation of strategic, gang-controlled favelas. Rumors that government forces would soon invade the sprawling favelas that composed the Complexo de Alemão spawned a tension that was palpable on the city's streets and over the airwaves. The rumors proved true and Rio de Janeiro held its breath as the government's military machinery and soldiers streamed into the city in preparations for what would be the largest favela occupation yet. Rio's residents stayed at home, retail stores barricaded their doors, the public buses stopped running, and people were glued to their television sets watching the mayhem live on Globo news.

On November 27, Niko, a Comando Vermelho (CV) boss in charge of a large *favela* on the city's north side, watched television coverage of armored tanks, heavily armed Brazilian soldiers, and uniformed police officers arrive at the entrance of the Complexo de Alemão, which served as his gang's headquarters. Niko sat less than two miles away from the action, hidden inside of a CV safe house with more than a dozen gang leaders from all corners of the city. The television coverage clearly showed that the force preparing to invade the Complexo de Alemão was more powerful than gang leadership had expected and they needed to decide how to react.

I spoke to Niko a few months after the invasion and he told me that there was a deep divide among the CV leaders in the safe house. Most thought that they should flee, but there was a very vocal minority arguing to fight back against the invaders and defend their territory.

These arguments quickly ended when images of tanks appeared on the television screen. Niko passed the edge of his hand over his palm as he told me, "I couldn't believe it. Those tanks cut through our barriers like a knife through butter, just like a knife through butter." In Niko's mind the coin had dropped and he yelled at his colleagues intent on fighting, "Are you kidding me? Go against the army? We are drug traffickers; we can't fight their tanks!"

Niko said his straightforward reasoning struck a chord in the room, and the decision was made to run from, not fight, the invading forces. The CV leaders sent word through the chain of command and hundreds, if not thousands, of gang members were suddenly on the run in Rio de Janeiro.

The day after the invasion, I sat in a storefront café watching fifty of those gang members run for their lives on television. I usually watched soccer games at the café, located in the middle-upper-class neighborhood Botafogo, but on that afternoon, the television showed Comando Vermelho members escaping en masse from their hideout in Complexo de Alemão. Every eye in the café was transfixed on the television, including those of the kitchen crew who had left pots boiling on the stove and dirty dishes in the sink to watch the events unfold.

The gang members escaped by following a dirt road leading out of the Complexo de Alemão and into an undeveloped jungle. The camera aboard the television station's helicopter zoomed in to show motorcycles piloted by other gang members appear at the scene to offer getaway rides to their escaping colleagues. As the motorcycles sped to safety under the weight of three and four people, a pickup truck joined the evacuation effort and was soon so packed with escaping CV members that the truck's doors could not close. Desperate to catch a ride, one young man lay face down on the hood of the truck and grabbed onto the windshield wipers as the vehicle kicked up dust and sped away.

Those who could not catch a ride scampered up the road on foot, until one of them suddenly fell to the ground, holding his upper thigh, writhing in pain. The young man had been hit by a sniper's bullet fired from a police helicopter hovering above the getaway route. The shot sent the rest of the gang members diving in to the bushes, and in the café my stomach tightened because I feared I was about to witness a massacre. But only one shot was fired, and after a very long thirty seconds passed dozens of young men emerged from their hiding places and resumed the exodus, sprinting up the hill while ducking at the waist, hoping not to get hit by the sniper's next bullet.

The massacre I expected never happened, and the CV members disappeared from the television screen. I wasn't the only one in the café surprised that the police fired only one shot. Once it became clear that the Comando Vermelho members would get away, a visibly agitated man in his late forties pushed back his stool from a table and stood up just a few feet from the television. Raising his hands over his head in disbelief, he yelled at the police snipers as if they could hear him: "Shoot! Shoot! Shoot! What are you doing? Shoot them! They are getting away!" He then lowered his hands to shoulder level and held his palms to the ceiling as he looked around the room, incredulously asking everyone in earshot, "What are they [the police] doing? Why aren't they shooting? Why aren't they shooting?"

I had watched numerous soccer games at this café and had seen many men use the same intonation, urgency, and hand gestures while jeering a poor pass or missed shot. But this time, the yells were not coming from a frustrated soccer fan, but a resident of Rio who was furious that the police did not kill the gang members when they had the chance.

Those days at the end of November provided a glimpse into the social world of a complicated city. When state forces successfully gained control of Complexo de Alemão they celebrated the victory by planting the Brazilian national flag and a flag representing the state of Rio de Janeiro on the highest, most visible spot in the neighborhood. This ritual, usually reserved for conquering armies, acknowledged a reality that Complexo de Alemão residents and Rio's police force have known for years: The Comando Vermelho, not the Brazilian state, had been the governing organization in the neighborhood. And the flags were meant to signal a regime change.

November 2010 was not the first time parts of Rio looked like a war zone. According to the nongovernmental organization Rio de Paz, 33,055 people were murdered in the state of Rio de Janeiro between 2007 and June 30, 2013.[1] During the same time period Rio's police force killed 5,412 people during official operations, making it one of the deadliest police forces on earth. Most of these killings were not streamed live on television like the events surrounding the Complexo de Alemão invasion, but the killings are hardly a secret. Bodies of young, darker-skinned men lying motionless in puddles of blood or being tossed into the backs of police vehicles have been a nightly fixture on Rio's local news for more than a decade. Not everyone cheers on the police like the man I saw in the café, but the public's outcry has been muted at best.

I asked the Rio de Paz leader, Pastor Antonio Carlos Costa, why there has been such a limited reaction from Rio's residents to the many thousands of people who have been killed by the police. The pastor pointed to *who* is being killed and said, "They are poor people, people with black skin, people considered killable. These are deaths that don't shock us; they don't make the Brazilian cry." The demographic trifecta described by Costa could also be used to describe most of the inmates in Rio's jails and prisons. Most of Rio's inmates are poor, darker-skinned young men—they are members of Rio de Janeiro's killable people.

Contested urban spaces like the Complexo de Alemão are crucial to understanding religious practice in prison because the majority of Rio's prison population were born and raised in these places before they were incarcerated. This chapter contextualizes Rio's prisons by framing the city's *favelas* and impoverished neighborhoods as the products of centuries of social exclusion and oppression. The social stigma placed upon *favela* residents has been exacerbated by the emergence of narco-gangs like the Comando Vermelho, and the city's homicide rates and number of police killings serve as evidence that poor, dark-skinned urban dwellers are treated by the state and larger society as less than full citizens.

FAVELAS IN THE MARVELOUS CITY

The Portuguese word *favela* has done well for itself over the last 115 years. Until 1895, it was just the common name for *Cnidoscolus quercifolius*, a scraggly tree that thrives on the hillsides of Rio de Janeiro and on the northeastern coast of Brazil. Today, *favela* might be the most globally recognized word in the Portuguese language. The word has a number of English translations—shantytown, ghetto, or slum— but it transitioned from describing a type of tree to describing a type of neighborhood when soldiers who finished fighting in the Canudos War marched into the city in 1897 to demand wages promised (but not paid) by the government (Madden 1993). Anticipating a lengthy wait, they set up a temporary encampment among the *favela* trees on a hillside. Eventually Rio's residents used the name of the tree to refer not only to the soldiers' tents and shelters, but also to the dozens of newly formed communities emerging along the edges of Rio de Janeiro.

Like many other cities in the Americas, Rio de Janeiro was built on the backs of slaves. Seven years before the camping soldiers arrived in the city, the Brazilian government passed the Golden Law freeing the country's one and a half million slaves. They were not a hidden, inconsequential group. More slaves arrived on Rio's shores than any other city in the Americas and by the middle of the nineteenth century over half of Rio's residents were slaves (Frank 2004). Slavery was woven into the fabric of every part of social life in nineteenth-century Brazil, and emancipation ruptured not only the labor market, but the housing market as well. The existing housing stock had no chance of absorbing the thousands of freed slaves. Because reparation or any sort of compensation package was not part of the Golden Law, the freed slaves built humble shelters on the city's vacant hillsides from whatever material they could find. They built the city's first *favelas*.

The soldiers from the Canudos War came and went, but the *favelas* named after their campsites continued to grow. In the early 1900s, yellow fever and a government-directed gentrification project pushed people from downtown into the growing hillside communities (Alves and Evanson 2011). The *favelas* increased in size and scope, stretching the city's footprint in every direction. By 1920, one hundred thousand people were living in what would be considered *favelas*, almost 10 percent of Rio's population. In the 1930s and 1940s another wave of migrants poured into Rio de Janeiro from the northeast, fleeing abject poverty and betting that they could find work and a better life in the nation's capital. These migrants continued to build the *favelas*.

The *favela* growth momentum did not stop in the following decades, even though Brazil went through a series of national upheavals, starting with President Juscelino Kubitschek's "fifty years of progress in five" campaign, which involved moving the capital from Rio to Brasilia in 1960. Just five years after the move, the military took control of the country in a coup and installed a dictatorship that ruled Brazil until it was replaced by a democratic government in 1985.

Democracy didn't immediately solve Brazil's problems; in fact, the out-of-control inflation and economic instability that followed the regime change made some Brazilians wonder why they had ousted the military dictatorship in the first place—at least it was predictable. In any case, Brazil survived the 1980s and early 1990s, an era now referred to as the "Lost Decade." The country enjoyed unprecedented economic growth under President Luiz Inacio Lula da Silva's—or "Lula's"—administration starting in 2002, but that growth was short-lived and Brazil hosted the 2016 Olympic Games in the midst of a deep recession and political turmoil.

During all of the macro-level changes in Brazil, Rio's *favelas* continued to grow. In each of the five decades between 1950 and 2000 *favela* growth outpaced growth in the rest of the city, and by 1996, more than one-third of Rio de Janeiro's population lived in either a *favela* or a government housing project (Leeds 1996; Perlman 2010). Estimates vary, but currently there are somewhere between six hundred and one thousand neighborhoods that are defined as *favelas*.[2]

Though the term *favela* is still the most common word used to describe poor neighborhoods in Rio de Janeiro, once again the language has changed and words like *comunidade* (community) and *morro* (hill) have entered the lexicon of Brazilian Portuguese to describe the city's

iconic hillside neighborhoods and peripheral suburbs that are characterized by concentrated poverty. Though the vocabulary continues to
evolve, the point crucial to this chapter is that from the moment the
Portuguese arrived in Guanabara Bay in 1502 until the time I collected
the data for this book, there has been a highly stigmatized, marginalized underclass in Rio de Janeiro living in places segregated by race
and class and characterized by social inequality.

Some scholars have argued that these places are not integrated into
the city, but Janet Perlman (1976) has argued for decades that these
places *are* integrated into the city because they "contribute their hard
work, their high hopes and their loyalties, but they do not benefit
from the goods and services of the system" (195). She contends that
"the favela dwellers are not economically and politically marginal but
exploited and repressed; not socially and culturally marginal but stigmatized and excluded from a closed social system. Rather than being
passively marginal in terms of their own attitudes and behavior, they
are being actively marginalized by the system and by public policy"
(195). Perlman argues that one hundred years after the Golden Law
was passed, the social hierarchy of nineteenth-century Rio de Janeiro
remained fully intact.

Despite persistent social and economic inequality, poverty has
decreased over the last decade in Rio de Janeiro. Comparatively, Rio's
favela residents enjoy access to material goods unimaginable to people
living in the urban slums of Sub-Saharan Africa, parts of Asia, and
even neighboring countries like Bolivia and Paraguay. A 2008 study
reported that 97 percent of *favela* residents had televisions, 94 percent
had refrigerators, and 55 percent walked around with cellphones in
their pockets (Alves and Evanson 2011). The national cash transfer
program, the Bolsa Familia, offered additional support to the city's
poorest residents, and hunger is no longer a pressing concern in Rio's
favelas.

But access to cellphones, TVs, and refrigerators does not mean that
poverty is disappearing in Rio, nor does it mean that the city's urban
poor are treated with dignity by the state and the rest of the city. After
returning to the *favelas* she studied in the early 1970s, Janet Perlman

(2010) argued, "The marginalization of Rio's poor is so extreme as to exclude them from the category of personhood" (316). Though income inequality in Rio de Janeiro has decreased since the start of the new millennium, the social stigma attached to *favela* residents has actually increased—the economic growth recently experienced in Rio has not been accompanied by a corresponding sense of dignity from residents of the *favelas*.

In a study on citizenship in Rio de Janeiro, residents of low-income neighborhoods cited dignity as the most important aspect of citizenship, not access to electronics or kitchen appliances (Wheeler 2003). One respondent summed up the sentiments of many members of Rio's marginalized underclasses by saying, "Dignity is everything for a citizen—and we have no dignity. We are treated like cattle in the clinics, on the buses, and in the shops. Only in rich neighborhoods are people treated with dignity" (41).

THE KILLABLE PEOPLE

Dignity is hard to quantify. What statistic could be used to measure it? Income figures don't help because there are poor people who live with dignity, while some who are wealthy do not, and vice versa. While measuring individual dignity is difficult, one number—5,412— captures the undignified attitude of the state toward a particular social group. Rio's police force killed 5,412 people between 2007 and 2013 in the state of Rio de Janeiro (according to Rio de Paz). More people are killed by Rio's police officers each year than are killed by police each year in the United States (Gabrielson, Grochowski Jones, and Sagara 2014). Brazil officially abolished capital punishment in 1889, but it is hard to argue that the punishment is no longer used when state employees killed more than one thousand people in the city of Rio de Janeiro alone (Garcia-Navarro 2014).

I first heard the term *seres matáves* (killable people) used to describe Rio's marginalized social classes at a talk by Dr. Ana Paula Miranda, an anthropologist at the Federal Fluminese University in Rio de

Janeiro. During a follow-up interview, when I asked her to explain the term in more detail, she said,

In Brazil when you talk about human rights people always ask, for *whom?* The police? The criminals? As if it were possible, as if it were necessary, to qualify who is human and who is not. This is the key issue to understand in this process. The killable people are not incorporated into the moral framework of citizenship; they are semi-citizens and therefore not deserving of the same rights.

Miranda argues that the killable people are understood through a perverse logic that grants different individuals in Rio different rights based on who they are. This concept is reinforced not only by the police but also by the family members of the victims of violence.

Miranda explained that when relatives of murder victims are interviewed in the media, they will often respond through tears by saying something like "my son was working, he wasn't a criminal—he did not deserve this." Miranda argues that statements like these reflect an underlying dark logic that determines whether a person deserves basic human rights (i.e., not to be shot) by asking if he or she is employed in the formal workforce. This thought process dictates that if a person is not working—or, worse yet, is employed by the drug gangs—they do not deserve the same protections as other citizens. The police killings in Rio are then tolerated because they occur among this specific group, *os seres matáves*, or the killable people. Miranda continued by stating that "if this absurd mortality rate happened in the middle class, there would be a different reaction. These are deaths that don't cause a commotion."

When I asked Pastor Antonio Carlos Costa of Rio de Paz to unpack the term, he emphasized the intersection of class and race:

Well, they are killable because they are poor. They are killable because they don't fit the middle-class standard of beauty. It is sad to say this, but they are killable because they are black and brown, so their deaths don't bother Rio de Janeiro's middle-class. The middle-class doesn't bear the brunt of today's violence because 80 percent of the violent deaths occur in poor communities in metropolitan Rio.

Costa characterized these deaths as ones that "don't make the Brazilian cry." The social science research backs their assessments (Cano 1997; Cano and Ribeiro 2007; Penglase 2005; Telles 2004).

MATTEOS ALVES DOS SANTOS, 2000–2014

Homicide statistics and terms like "killable people" are useful in framing the scale of the daily violence in Rio. Focusing on the events surrounding one of these killings reveals how some people are killed simply for *who* they are.

On July 11, 2014, Officers Fábio Magalhães Ferreira and Vinícius Lima Vieira patrolled Avenida Presidente Vargas, a historic, bustling avenue that cuts through Rio's downtown core. A dashboard camera recently installed in their squad SUV was turned on and working properly, so the officers' entire shift (all but ten minutes) would be recorded and later leaked to the press. The video footage provided a detailed account of one of the police killings from 2014, and the images gave a tragic glimpse of what it looks like when citizens are treated without dignity or considered as killable.

According to the video footage recovered from the police car, at 9:21 A.M. the officers spotted two dark-skinned teenage boys who fit the description of young men suspected of a recent robbery in downtown Rio. Officer Lima grabbed his assault rifle, left the parked car, and pursued the boys on foot. Fifteen minutes later, he returned to the car to place a handcuffed teen, fourteen-year-old Matteos Alves dos Santos, into the back of the police SUV. Once Matteos was in the trunk, Officer Lima left the squad car again to pursue the other suspect. According to the video footage, ten minutes later a second suspect was arrested and put into the back of the SUV next to Matteos. In what was a surprise to Officer Vieira who had stayed by the squad car, Officer Lima had arrested a third young man and locked him in the back of the SUV alongside the two robbery suspects. When Officer Vieira asked his partner who the third person in the back was, Officer Lima told him that the young man was "standing and staring" at him during the arrest, so he pointed at him and told the security guards standing close by to "grab that one, too."

When the two officers drove away from the scene of the arrest, there were three handcuffed teenagers in the back of the vehicle: two suspected of theft and one accused of staring. After the arrests the officers had to decide what to do with the three suspects. At 9:49 A.M., Officer Lima wiped his forehead and asked his partner, "Should we take them up there?" Officer Ferreira nodded and responded, "Unload the gun a bit?"

"Up there" meant Morro do Sumaré, an isolated jungle area thirty minutes from downtown Rio. Data recovered from the police car's GPS system revealed that the officers drove directly from the location of the last arrest to Morro do Sumaré. After a half-hour drive, the police officers arrived at Morro do Sumaré, where they followed a dirt road deep into the jungle and away from any witnesses. The officers stopped the car at 10:20 A.M. to release the young man they had arrested for "standing and staring." As Officer Lima closed the tailgate on the two remaining detainees, he told them, "We haven't even started beating you yet and you are already crying? Stop crying! You are crying too much! Be a man!" The police officers then drove deeper into the jungle and video footage recovered from the dashboard camera clearly shows the silhouettes of the two young men sitting in the back of the vehicle.

At 10:32 A.M., the video feed from the dashboard camera inexplicably stops. According to the car's GPS system the police officers had parked the car on a secluded turnoff adjacent to a thick, difficult-to-access jungle area. As suddenly as the video footage cuts out at 10:32 A.M., it reappears at 10:42 A.M. But when the video footage reappeared, the squad car was no longer climbing Morro do Sumaré, it was descending and returning to the city. More importantly the silhouettes of the two boys who had been sitting in the back of the SUV were no longer there.

On July 16, five days after Officer Lima and Officer Vieira made the arrests, the body of Matteos Alves dos Santos was found in the jungle. He had been shot execution-style in the head. He was fourteen years old. The other boy in the back of the car had been shot as well, but unlike his friend Matteos, he did not die from the bullets fired into his body. The young man's identity is being kept hidden in fear of retribution from the police, but according to his account, he was shot in his leg and back and was left in the jungle assumed to be dead. Amazed he was still alive, the boy waited until he was sure that the officers had left the area before crawling out of the jungle to get help.

Once the video footage was posted online, the two officers were arrested, but the police department's Internal Affairs investigator refused to make a definitive statement on the situation and implied his hands were tied because of the missing footage. "Since we lost the images, we can't really tell what the officer did or did not do" (*Globo* 2014).

The most unsettling aspect of the footage was how routine the entire affair seemed to the officers and how casually they handled what appears to be a weekday morning execution of a fourteen-year-old boy and the attempted murder of a fifteen-year-old. After the officers made the arrests in downtown Rio they never discussed bringing them to jail or even questioned whether or not they had arrested the right pair of darker-skinned young men. The officers not only treated Matteos Alves dos Santos and his friend as if they were less than full citizens, they treated them as if they were less than human. They treated them as killable.

It is impossible to know how the city would react if the nearly one thousand people killed each year by the police were lighter-skinned and middle-class or if Matteos had been born in Ipanema instead of Maré, a *favela*. Protests surrounding the 2014 World Cup and the 2016 Olympic Games have shown that Brazilians are willing and able to take to the streets to protest social issues they feel strongly about. Thousands marched on the streets of downtown Rio de Janeiro to demand higher salaries for teachers in May 2015. In June 2014, tens of thousands of residents in Rio protested in the streets against the perceived corruption and misallocation of funds in Brazil's preparation for the World Cup.

The protests around government spending and corruption have been largely middle-class affairs.[3] There has been nothing close to this sort of outrage or public disapproval in response to the killing of poor citizens by police or to the tens of thousands of people whose lives have been lost to violence over the last decade. As Miranda said, "These are deaths that don't cause a commotion."

THE COMANDO VERMELHO: A PARALLEL POWER BORN IN PRISON

There are a number of variables that have contributed to the violent deaths and increased marginalization suffered by Rio's poor. Janet Perlman (2010) points to a combination of poverty, government indifference to the needs of the poor, easy access to high-powered weapons, demand for narcotics, and highly organized narco-gangs. Though no one variable can be blamed for all of the violence, the emergence and growth of narco-gangs like the Comando Vermelho have inarguably exacerbated the marginality of Rio's poor neighborhoods and directly caused the deaths of thousands of young men in the city. Gangs are particularly important to this project because of the power they hold inside prisons and the intimate relationship they have with the city's Pentecostals.

In the late 1970's the Brazilian military dictatorship decided to house both political prisoners and street criminals inside the same cellblocks at Candido Mendes on Ilha Grande, the Brazilian equivalent of Alcatraz. If the dictatorship could have somehow seen twenty years into the future, they would have thought twice about that plan. The volatile mixture of dissidents and streetwise convicts inside the prison spawned one of the most violent and tightly organized narco-gangs in the world, the Comando Vermelho.

In the social scientific literature on prisons, the "less eligibility" principle stipulates that if prisons are going to serve as a deterrent to crime, conditions inside the prisons must be worse than those afforded to members of the lowest social class. I am uncertain if this theoretical principle guided the Brazilian military dictatorship's administration of prisons, but regardless the government was wildly successful in creating a prison environment that offered worse living conditions than were found in Rio's poorest *favelas*.

Conditions in Candido Mendes were oppressive, violent, and anarchic. I spoke with Domingo, an ex-inmate who was incarcerated in Candido Mendes in the late 1970s and early 1980s. He told me,

> When I got to Candido Mendes, it was every man for himself. There were no gangs; the prison hadn't been divided into gangs yet. Everyone was mixed together on the floor and slept on thin mats. The cells barely fit ten or fifteen people, but they put in fifty or seventy of us in there, piled on top of each other on the floor.... There were fights all of the time and people destroying each other. It was pure destruction.

The political prisoners in Candido Mendes may have been amateurs at street crime, but they were experts in organizing against an oppressive state. This was a useful skill in prison, and the political prisoners shifted their immediate focus from toppling the national government to improving conditions inside the cellblocks at Candido Mendes. Prior to the arrival of the political prisoners in the cells, the inmates took out their frustrations on each other, exacerbating the misery of the brutal living conditions—"pure destruction," as Domingo described it. The political prisoners saw the daily inmate-on-inmate violence and looming unpredictability as something that dramatically reduced the quality of life for the entire prison population and hindered the ability of prisoners to organize and act collectively against the brutally indifferent administration.

In 1979, a group composed of both political prisoners and common criminals coalesced and initiated a major prison riot in Candido Mendes. The group called itself the Falange Vermelho (Red Phalanx) and killed any of their fellow prisoners who refused to participate in the riot or recognize their burgeoning group's leadership role behind bars (Penglase 2014).

Though many of the political prisoners were jailed because of their opposition to the military dictatorship, they did not pursue democratic rule through their gang. The gang was merciless toward its opponents and rose to power quickly, maintaining control of the cellblocks with violence that would have made even the military dictatorship a bit queasy. The Falange Vermelho, which would soon change its name to the Comando Vermelho (Red Command), set up its own dictatorship inside the prison and governed the space by implementing and enforcing a set of laws to dictate almost every aspect of daily life in the cellblocks.

Domingo told me that the gang's ascendance made life more predictable and less violent inside of the prison:

> Conditions improved the moment the gang was founded, because they put a stop to some of the things that were happening in there. Prisoners stopped robbing each other, raping each other, you know.... The Red Phalanx started to kill the people who did these sorts of things inside of prison.

The laws implemented and enforced by the CV prohibited unauthorized inmate-on-inmate violence, punished sexual assaults by death, and demanded unwavering loyalty to the gang. It shifted the balance of power inside prison away from the state and toward the inmates, fundamentally changing daily life inside of prison.

As the Comando Vermelho grew in strength, the organization set its sights on establishing itself outside of the cellblocks. The CV entered Rio's *favelas* as affiliated inmates were released and returned to their old neighborhoods. The gang largely abandoned the leftist political agenda imported by the political prisoners and focused instead on monetary gain. Comando Vermelho members began to form a loosely organized crime network on the streets to rob banks, kidnap for ransom, and enter the small-scale marijuana distribution market.

The early 1980s was a fortuitous time to enter organized crime in Rio de Janeiro—as the military dictatorship was on its way out, powder cocaine was on its way in. Quantities of processed cocaine previously unheard of were suddenly available from neighboring South American countries and the domestic demand for the product was exploding (Arias 2006). Leaders in the Comando Vermelho recognized that the profits from cocaine trade had the potential to be many times greater than what could be grabbed during a bank heist or negotiated from a kidnapping, so they transitioned into cocaine traffic in the early 1980s.

The cocaine trade differed from other sorts of organized criminal ventures because it had a much higher upfront cost and required secure distribution networks in order to sell the drug. Desmond Arias (2006) argues that the cocaine business necessitated a deeper, more violent presence in Rio's impoverished and socially isolated neighborhoods:

> Ultimately, the nature of the cocaine trade itself and the increasing resources needed to defend turf probably also contributed to the growth and consolidation of gangs. The marijuana trade had a relatively low overhead and moved small amounts of cash. As bribes grew more costly, narcotics prices went up, and the weapons needed to defend those narcotics grew more expensive. As a result, traffickers needed to organize themselves more efficiently and build stronger ties with other criminals who could give them material support. (29)

Comando Vermelho members knew that the *favelas* were socially and geographically isolated from the rest of the city. The state's chronic absence in these neighborhoods, combined with a collective distrust of the police, made the *favelas* ripe for an alternative governing force. Elizabeth Leeds (1996) summarized the growth of the gangs: "Parallel power structures thus have arisen in a space left empty by the lack of truly protective state structures" (78).

The gang's entry point to the *favelas* was through powerful community associations that operated as the de facto local government in these spaces. The Comando Vermelho was able to co-opt these organizations by bribing community association leadership, promising to invest resources from the drug traffic into the community and something equally enticing to community residents—a governing power that treated residents with dignity.

Through cocaine sales the CV's profits and membership grew. The gang chose to headquarter the packaging and distribution components of their growing drug enterprise in Rio's *favelas* because they offered important strategic advantages. The neighborhoods were difficult to enter, rarely patrolled by the police and offered hidden spaces in which to package and store illegal narcotics. These neighborhoods also provided an untapped labor pool in the thousands of young men who were largely excluded from the formal economy. The Comando Vermelho offered *favela* teenagers fast money, a sense of belonging, and the sort of respect that comes with carrying a weapon. Business boomed, and by 1985, the CV controlled over 70 percent of the cocaine business in Rio de Janeiro. In 2005 over half of the city's *favela* residents lived in neighborhoods controlled by the Comando Vermelho.

Much as it did in the prisons, the gang established its power by instituting and enforcing its own set of rules in the neighborhoods. The gang's presence in these neighborhoods towered over the state's presence. Gang rules trumped anything put forth by the state for the simple fact that there were consequences for breaking the gang's laws. Petty crimes like purse snatching or shoplifting inside the *favela* might not attract the attention of the police, but the gang leaders would punish the offender by shooting them in the hand or some other form of violence. Dishonorable crimes like sexual assaults or the gang's cardinal sin of talking to the police were punished by death. Gangs began to take on more responsibilities traditionally held by the state, and *favela* residents had to consult with the gang even for such mundane tasks as making renovations to their homes or holding a birthday party in the street.

The rise of the narco-gangs changed the nature of marginalization of neighborhoods in Rio de Janeiro. As Ben Penglase (2014) argues, "The CV is an example of, and a main contributor to, the new ways that favela residents are integrated into and yet excluded from larger socio-economic systems" (120). Residents who lived in gang-controlled neighborhoods were often assumed to be involved in illegal activity, or affiliated with the gang, cutting residents' job opportunities even further. State provisions, police, schools, and healthcare barely existed in the *favelas* before the gangs took control, and their arrival nearly thirty years ago has only made matters worse.

SIGHTS AND SOUNDS OF A *FAVELA*

What does a CV neighborhood look like from the inside? The Comando Vermelho controlled dozens of neighborhoods while I collected data for this project, and although I did not come close to visiting all of the Comando Vermelho–controlled spaces in Rio de Janeiro, I spent a lot of time in these neighborhoods visiting inmates' families and meeting with pastors working in these areas. When they first arrived as powerful forces in the *favelas*, the gangs promised an alternative governing body that would uphold the dignity of neighborhood residents. Though the gang has been wildly profitable over the last three decades it has profoundly failed to deliver on its governance promises. What I saw was a power that intensified the existing oppression and social exclusion.

I vividly remember the first time I entered a Comando Vermelho–controlled *favela*, especially the red hand-painted stripes on the Uzi held by the teenager guarding the neighborhood's entrance. Both residents and visitors had to enter the area on foot and pass by an armed guard[4] because the Comando Vermelho had installed a series of fifty-five-gallon metal drums filled with concrete across the street entrances. The metal drums turned the *favela* into a "gated community" and cut off the neighborhood from surrounding areas. Fire trucks, ambulances, and taxis could not service the neighborhood because of the barricades; instead, maintaining a profitable drug trade has been the driving force behind the gang's strategic decisions, endangering and isolating community residents as the cost of doing business.

On my first visit to this neighborhood I accompanied a deacon from a local Assembly of God Church, a former crack user who recently converted to Pentecostalism, and a pastor who had a good reputation with the gang as a result of his prison ministry. I visited this community regularly, but never alone. I always went with someone whom I trusted, usually a pastor, but always with someone who was known and trusted by the guys holding the guns. The Assembly of God deacon had been a CV member before he converted to Pentecostalism. The gunshot wound he suffered in the late 1990s left him with a severe limp, which set our group's pace as we walked through the neighborhood. Our visit was approved by gang leadership, so once we passed by the young man with the painted gun, the four of us leaned against a railing and waited for our meeting.

From my spot on the railing, I stared wide-eyed at the scene in front of me. To my immediate right, there were over a dozen young men, mostly teenagers, scattered on top of three couches surrounding an enormous flat-screen television. The gang's "soldiers" sat in the open-air lounge protected from the sun by a plastic tarp that hung from the telephone poles, which allowed them to watch soccer highlights and smoke marijuana in the shade. If wasn't for the assault rifles resting on their laps they would have looked like any other group of high school boys in Rio. Though I didn't recognize anyone, I might have seen some of these young men on television running from the police helicopter in the café a few months earlier.

Looking over my left shoulder, I had a clear view of the economic engine that powered the gang's control of the neighborhood, the *boca de fumo* (mouth of smoke), or the drug distribution point. The drugs for sale were organized into four cardboard boxes on top of a wobbly kitchen table that looked strangely out of place in such a nondomestic setting. Two of the boxes held prepackaged packets of marijuana branded with the gang's logo and corresponding price. The other boxes contained doses of powder cocaine, branded and priced according to quantity. Three men, much older than the glassy-eyed teenagers on the sofa, stood directly behind the table with their backs against a concrete wall. Two of them held formidable-looking automatic weapons in their arms and stood behind the other man, who squeezed a softball-sized wad of cash in his hands.

Customers formed a line in front of the table under the watchful eye of the CV men and their guns. When the buyers arrived at the boxes, some of them held up the small plastic packets of cocaine or marijuana in the sunlight for inspection, the way a fussy shopper might examine an apple in the grocery store. Once the customer found something suitable, he or she handed over cash, and it was added to the growing stack of bills in the gang member's hands. After the purchase, most customers pocketed the drugs and went on their way, but others snorted or lit their purchase within a few feet of the table. The scene was surreal to me, but to the dozens of community residents who passed us returning from their jobs, this was the backdrop of their daily commute.

Thousands of young men have died in turf battles with rival gangs and at the hands of the police in order to establish these open-air drug markets. Domestic drug sales are the lifeblood of the organization and there was a *boca de fumo* in nearly every gang-controlled neighborhood during my time in Rio. Not every *boca* was set up exactly like the one I described, but the others I saw and heard about operated in a similar fashion. In order for the gang to conduct their business in this manner, they needed to regulate who enters and exits the neighborhood and to ensure that local residents did not cooperate with the police. This sort of drug trade requires a parallel power to govern the space around the point of sale with the ability to punish noncompliers.

It was a hot, windless day and the marijuana smoke hung heavy in the air as the four of us continued to wait. Sexually explicit lyrics from a funk song blasted so loudly from the outdoor sound system behind us that I had to yell directly into the ears of my companions to communicate. The song's chorus, which was simply the name of a sex act repeated over and over to a bass line, pummeled the air. As we stood watching, I saw the pastor's eyes follow a father leading his seven- or eight-year-old daughter by the hand past the sound system, drug stand, and sofas. The pastor shook his head, bit his upper lip, and leaned over to tell me, "No father should have to pass through this sort of humiliation." This wasn't the first time the father had to make this walk, and he knew to keep his head down and avoid eye contact. His daughter assumed the same posture, and the two of them walked by us hand-in-hand with their eyes pointed directly to the ground.

The image of the father and daughter with their heads bowed and staring at their feet as they walk through their neighborhood is an example of what Perlman (2010) refers to as the *mundo de medo* (the sphere of fear) that has arisen in neighborhoods controlled by narco-gangs:

> The violence and its twin offshoots—fear and distrust—not only prevent the use of public space but also diminish socializing among friends and relatives, reduce membership in community organizations, weaken trust among neighbors, and erode community unity. The flow of information about jobs, programs, and all manner of opportunities that was spread through informal community networks has dried up, and the coping mechanisms based on *mutirao* (mutual aid) are barely intact. (194)

Perlman compared statistics from the data she collected in Rio's favelas in 1969 with the data she collected in 2001 and found that there were substantial decreases in membership in community organizations (not including churches), the frequency of social visits, trust among residents, and unity in neighborhoods. The arrival of narco-gangs has increased the marginality of Rio's *favelas* as they have prevented businesses and jobs in the formal economy from entering these neighborhoods. Moreover, the fear they have instilled in these communities has strained interpersonal relationships and eroded networks useful to surviving urban poverty.

RIO'S PRISONS: *FAVELAS* BEHIND BARS

Favelas are places that are fundamentally tied to Rio's prisons. These neighborhoods supply most of the people in the prison population, and the prisons themselves are the manifestations of the inequality and oppression rooted in centuries of history. The inhumane conditions inside Rio's prisons and especially the jails reflect how this segment of the city has historically been treated by the state and the middle and upper classes as a whole. Rio's prison cells are made for and filled by the killable people.

Homicide rates and the number of people killed by the police each year are other ways to illustrate how a social class is treated as less than full citizens; so are the stories like the tragic murder of Matteos Alves dos Santos. Unequal access to the prison system is another. For decades, members of the middle and upper classes who have committed crimes have been provided a variety of ways to avoid being sent to the cellblocks of Salgado and Cinza. Brazilian politicians have been granted a special judicial standing that has all but ensured that they do not serve prison time, even for crimes like murder, extortion, embezzlement, and bribery. A 2013 ruling in Brazil's largest corruption case may change the impunity granted to lawmakers, but the legal system has been constructed to guarantee that the political elite do not face the same consequences as members of lower social classes who commit identical crimes.

State employees who are not elected officials do not enjoy the same untouchable status as the politicians, but if a police officer or a member of the fire department or military is convicted of a crime, they are sent to different prisons where the conditions do not compare to the institutions I studied. They are able to avoid these prisons not because of what they did, but because of who they are. Even a college degree—something that very few *favela* residents have—grants access to a different prison if the person holding the degree is arrested.

The loopholes in the system benefit not just state employees and elected officials. Offenders with enough money and the right connections can and do buy their way out of incarceration through bribes to the police and government officials. I witnessed this happen in Salgado when the son of a European businessman was sent to jail for a drug offense. The young man's parents were called into the jail and had a private meeting with the guards and arresting officers. Though others arrested for an identical crime spent weeks and often months waiting in the jail to receive their sentences, this young man was released within hours of his arrival. He never spent a night in Salgado.

These formal and informal escape clauses, combined with discriminatory policing tactics as well as harsh penalties for involvement in gang-related drug trafficking, all but ensure that prison beds and jail cells are reserved for Rio's killable people.

CHAPTER 3

PENTECOSTALISM

THE FAITH OF THE KILLABLE PEOPLE

Leandro do Nascimento managed the Comando Vermelho's cocaine and marijuana trade in the Minerlândia neighborhood located on the north side of Rio de Janeiro. He was among the CV leaders hiding out in Complexo de Alemão when the police and military forces invaded in November 2010. Leandro saw the tanks roll in like everyone else in the neighborhood, but he opted for a different escape strategy than his colleagues. Leandro was wanted for two homicides, including the murder of a police officer—turning himself in was not an option. Not wanting to take his chances dodging bullets during his escape, he swapped his surf shorts, sunglasses, and flashy jewelry for a suit, tie, and polished leather shoes. He tucked a Bible under his arm to complete the outfit then tried to walk out of the neighborhood disguised as a Pentecostal pastor.[1]

Leandro knew that Pentecostalism was by far the most widely practiced faith in Complexo de Alemão. Thousands of gang members had converted to Pentecostalism over the last two decades. As Pastor Antonio Carlos Costa told me, "There is not one Pentecostal church located in a poor neighborhood in Rio de Janeiro that does not have at least one converted gang member in the pews." Rio's *favelas* are filled with Pentecostals, and since many of them, like Leandro, are young men with dark skin, so he thought he would try to blend in with the urban scenery.

Marina Maggessi, the chief of intelligence officer of Rio de Janeiro's police department, said that, in the *favelas*, "drug traffic is many times the only institution that they [*favela* residents] know. They don't have family, religion, government, and the police is seen as enemy number one."[2] While it is true that narco-gangs are the most powerful institution in many *favelas*, the idea that residents are not also involved in other institutions like family or religion is simply a fallacy. Leandro knew that the neighborhood was full of Pentecostal churches.

Still, the plan didn't work as Leandro hoped, and he was arrested at the police checkpoint. Posing as a Pentecostal was not as easy as he anticipated. I don't use Leandro's failed escape attempt to suggest that gang members adopt a Pentecostal identity as a disingenuous scheme to fool the police or the rest of society; instead I am illustrating just how widespread the faith is in the *favelas* and how the two identities are active in the same spaces and social groups. In Rio de Janeiro, Pentecostalism is strongest among the city's poor, and in the *favelas* it is the most widely practiced religion.

The previous chapter focused on the most dominant force in Rio's *favelas*, the narco-gang, and conceptualized the gang members and the residents of the city's low-income neighborhoods as *os seres matáves*, the killable people. This chapter examines Pentecostalism, another powerful nonstate entity that is strongest in the same spaces where the gang is strongest. In Rio de Janeiro, Pentecostalism is the faith of the killable people. Thus, understanding Pentecostalism is crucial to comprehending not only Rio's low-income neighborhoods, but the city's prisons as well. This chapter traces the spread of Pentecostalism from early twentieth-century Los Angeles to the *favelas* of twenty-first-century Rio de Janeiro, and it explores the complex interactions among the two most prominent institutions in Rio's *favelas*: the narco-gang and the Pentecostal church.

PENTECOSTALISM

Pentecostalism is a relatively young movement in Christianity that traces its roots to a converted barn on Azusa Street in early twentieth-century Los Angeles. The meteoric rise of the faith has been well documented by historians and social scientists and though this chapter will not provide a blow-by-blow account of the origins and global growth of the movement, there are important characteristics of the faith that have been present from the beginning which help to explain why it is the dominant form of religious expression in Rio de Janeiro's *favelas* as well as its prisons.

Pentecostalism arguably began in 1905 with an ironic scene in Houston, Texas. William Seymour was sitting by himself in a hallway at Houston Bible School, listening to lectures through a propped-open door. Today, Seymour is known as the founder of the global Pentecostal movement, which makes him one of the most influential Christians to ever live. In the mid-1990s the theologian Harvey Cox (1995) credited Seymour with starting "a spiritual hurricane that already touched nearly half a billion people, and an alternative vision of the human future whose impact may only be in its earliest stages today" (65). The faith has continued to grow substantially since Cox made his claim. But in the early twentieth century, scholars were not waxing poetically about Seymour's impact on the world. In fact, Seymour wasn't deemed worthy to sit in the same classroom as the other students at Houston Bible College because he was an African American.

Seymour was fascinated with the role of the Holy Spirit in Christian practice, and he asked Charles Parham, the founder of Houston Bible School and one of the foremost Holiness preachers in the country during the early 1900s, whether he could attend classes at the school. Parham was an unapologetic segregationist who had an affinity for the Ku Klux Klan, and the thought of having a black student sitting in his classroom was unimaginable. Yet instead of refusing Seymour outright, Parham offered a compromise and put the chair for Seymour in the hallway.

The irony of Seymour's exclusion from the classroom seems obvious, given his role in launching Pentecostalism. On the other hand, the image of Seymour sitting in the hallway may not be ironic at all; rather, it serves as a perfect emblem for the movement. Since its inception Pentecostalism has been composed primarily of people sitting in a chair in a metaphorical hallway. From William Seymour forward, Pentecostalism has been the strongest among the poor, ethnic minorities, immigrants, urban migrants, and others living on the margins of their societies.

William Seymour was born in Louisiana in 1870 to former slaves. He grew up during some of the worst postemancipation years for African Americans in the South. Just like in twenty-first-century Rio de Janeiro, there were "killable people" in the United States in the early 1900s, and Seymour was one of them. From the time he was twelve years old in 1882 until the time Seymour tried to enroll in Houston Bible School in 1905, more than two thousand black men had been lynched in the United States.[3] Charles Parham wasn't the first or likely the worst racist Seymour had encountered.

But Seymour didn't last long sitting in the hallway listening to Parham's lectures. He was invited to preach in the growing town of Los Angeles, so like tens of thousands of other Americans in the early 1900s, Seymour packed his bags and headed to California. He started preaching with the church that invited him to Los Angeles, but as a result of a theological dispute with the host pastor, the relationship soured and he was asked to leave the church. Undeterred by the rejection, Seymour started preaching on his own inside living rooms and on the patios of houses in the residential area north of Temple Street. At the time, the neighborhood was home primarily to African American domestic workers and laborers. It was early twentieth-century Los Angeles's version of Rio's twenty-first-century *favelas*.

For years, Seymour had been studying the Bible and praying for an experience with the Holy Spirit like the scene described in the biblical account in Acts 2. He wanted an intimate encounter with the Holy Spirit that included speaking in tongues, but the experience had been elusive. On April 12, 1906, it finally happened. Seymour reported being filled by the Holy Spirit and for the first time started to pray aloud in a language that seemed to be from another world.

Word traveled quickly among Angelenos, primarily African Americans, who were interested in this newly arrived preacher and the mysterious and mystical Christian practice he promoted. People flooded to the homes where Seymour preached and prayed, and within days the living rooms and porches could not contain the crowds. Out of necessity Seymour moved his group of followers into a dilapidated, vacant warehouse at 312 Azusa Street on the edge of downtown Los Angeles.

The building on Azusa Street was rough. At one point it had hosted an African Methodist Episcopal church, but most recently it had been used as a horse stable. The wooden structure had low ceilings and smelled like a barn. Since Seymour's followers didn't know how long this outpouring of the Holy Spirit would last, they didn't want to waste time renovating the structure. The building didn't have stained-glass windows, a pipe organ, or a steeple, but it served as the launching pad for a movement that would change the trajectory of global Christianity.

Worship services were held three times a day, seven days a week, for over three years. Sometimes one service carried over into the next and never really stopped, so worshippers occupied the building twenty-four hours a day. Seymour and others preached, prayed, and sang as they felt the Holy Spirit lead them. The whole scene seemed chaotic to some, but others were drawn to it. Soon after the doors opened, the building was regularly filled with more than one thousand worshippers, many of whom made sounds that could not be heard in any other Protestant church in the United States.

William Durham, who would later become a Pentecostal leader in the Midwest and eventually mentor missionaries headed to Brazil, made the pilgrimage to Los Angeles to visit Seymour's church in early 1907. Durham arrived in Los Angeles skeptical of a form of Christianity that seemed to emphasize emotion over reason. He changed his tune after attending a service:

> The first thing that impressed me was the love and unity that prevailed in the meeting, and the heavenly sweetness that filled the very air that I breathed. I want to say right here, that I have attended many large Holiness camp meetings and conventions, but I never felt the power and glory that I felt in Azusa Street Mission, and when about twenty persons joined in singing the "Heavenly Chorus," it was the most ravishing and unearthly music that ever fell on mortal ears. (Davenport 2008, 176)

Like many of the participants who attended the services, Durham *felt* something inside 312 Azusa Street. The palpable emotion in the room and the worshippers' belief that God was actually present made this place special to attendees and convinced people to make the pilgrimage to downtown Los Angeles from every corner of the country. People were not traveling across the United States and in some cases the world simply to increase their intellectual knowledge about God; they could do that in nearly any decently sized city. Rather, people boarded trains heading west and made the journey to Los Angeles because they wanted to experience God and feel the Holy Spirit.

Glossolalia, or speaking in tongues, was one of the defining features of the worship services during the Azusa Street Revival. The practice was important to Seymour because it was a sign of the baptism in the Holy Spirit described in the book of Acts in the Bible. The experience of speaking in tongues varied among participants at the Azusa Street services. Some reported they could suddenly speak a living language like French or Yiddish, while others spoke in a language that was unintelligible without an interpreter. William Durham described the first time he spoke in tongues:

> On Friday evening, March 1, His mighty power came over me, until I jerked and quaked under it for about three hours. It was strange and wonderful and yet glorious. He worked my whole body, one section at a time, first my arms, then my limbs, then my body, then my head, then my face, then my chin, and finally at 1 A.M., Saturday, March 2, after being under the power for three hours, He finished the work on my vocal organs, and spoke through me in unknown tongues. I arose, perfectly conscious outwardly and inwardly that I was fully baptized in the Holy Ghost, and the devil can never tempt me to doubt it. (Synan 2003, 54)

Hundreds of people reported having experiences similar to Durham's. Some said that they were filled with the Holy Spirit and started speaking in tongues on the dusty road outside of the building as they approached for the first time.

Not everyone in Los Angeles was impressed with what they observed. A reporter for the *Los Angeles Times* offered a very different vision of Seymour's congregation:

> Breathing strange utterances and mouthing a creed which it seems no sane mortal could understand, the newest religious sect has started in Los Angeles. Meetings are held in a tumble-down shack on Azusa Street ... and devotees of the weird doctrine practice the most fanatical rites, preach the wildest theories and work themselves into a state of mad excitement in their peculiar zeal. Colored people and a sprinkling of whites compose the congregation, and night is made hideous in the neighborhood by the howlings of the worshippers who spend hours swaying forth and back in a nerve-racking attitude of prayer and supplication. (Billingsly 2008, 16)

Though rarely stated as directly as it was in the *Times* reporter's dispatch, criticisms of Pentecostalism have remained consistent for the last one hundred years. Both fellow Christians and social commentators have ridiculed Pentecostalism as a faith unhinged that relies on irrational emotion and is practiced by socially undesirable, unstable zealots.

Despite the criticism, speaking in tongues remained central to the religious practice. Initially Seymour pointed to it as the primary evidence that God's spirit was present, but over time, he highlighted something just as strange and rare as the evidence of God at work. There were African Americans, whites, Hispanics, and Asians worshipping together under the same roof, which made the congregation at Azusa Street wildly unique for its time. When Seymour first transitioned from preaching on the front steps of houses to the building on Azusa Street, the congregation was predominantly African American, but curiosity quickly spread across racial lines.

Seymour's leadership team was multiracial, which put some white men directly under his authority. This, maybe more so than the glossolalia, was radically countercultural at the time. Los Angeles was experiencing a population boom and was selling itself to the rest of the country as an Aryan Utopia (Davis 2006). The Azusa Street meetings, composed of ethnic minorities practicing Christianity in a way that looked very different than what was done in the established churches in the rest of the country, was not the kind of utopianism that many of the city leaders wanted to encourage.

The Pentecostal historian Vinson Synan argues that the multiracial composition of the congregation at Azusa Street was not only unique for Christianity in the United States, but also unique for all modern Christianity: "From that day on I would say Pentecostalism has had more crossing of ethnic boundaries than any movement in the world in Christianity (Allen 2006)." Frank Bartleman, a pastor who attended the revival, boldly proclaimed, "The color line was washed away in the blood of Jesus." (Hunter 2006, 169).

The Azusa Street Revival burned brightly, but like most roaring fires, the movement couldn't maintain its intensity forever, and the Azusa mission was reduced to smoldering coals in just over three years. Seymour's ministry was losing momentum. Because Pentecostal churches and leaders were emerging across the country, making the trek to California was unnecessary for people interested in the faith. Seymour's role as a national leader was diminished by a series of theological disputes and personality clashes within his church. But the knockout punch came from an unlikely source—William Durham, the preacher who spoke so positively about his first visit to 312 Azusa Street.

Durham had a life-changing experience in Seymour's worship service and remained in Los Angeles to preach and guide the revival while Seymour was away preaching in other cities. But Durham had reservations about Seymour's theological emphasis on the role of the Holy Spirit and eventually left the church. But he did not leave by himself; most of Azusa's white congregants followed Durham out the door and into his new church, which provided a space for white Pentecostals to speak in tongues in an all-white setting. Bartleman may have been more accurate if he had claimed that the color line had been temporarily "covered up" instead of "washed away," because the stain of racism still remained just under the surface.

Seymour's church, and Seymour himself, never fully recovered from the loss of the congregation's white members. Because Seymour's theology had come to emphasize that the multiracial nature of the congregation was the sign of the Holy Spirit's presence, as opposed to simply speaking in tongues, he was disheartened when once again he was preaching to a nearly all-black congregation. Though Seymour's church had started with a bang it ended with a whimper. He died in 1922 as the leader of a small and shrinking congregation. It was unlikely he had any idea of the impact he had made on modern Christianity.

The Azusa Street Revival is now understood as the starting point of global Pentecostalism. Seymour and his ramshackle church played the same role as rocket boosters do on a space shuttle. Full of fuel at the beginning, after ignition, the boosters propel the space shuttle from the ground up through the atmosphere. Once the shuttle has been launched and can fly by itself, the empty boosters are ejected from the craft and no longer have a role to play in the shuttle's voyage.

MOVING ON FROM LOS ANGELES

Pentecostalism wasn't confined to Azusa Street for long. Even though Seymour's church wilted under the pressure of theological discord and the strains of segregation, the movement spread to all corners of the United States, spreading from city to city. The movement spoke (and still speaks) most strongly to the city dweller, and there were millions more urban residents in the United States when Seymour opened the doors on Azusa Street than there had been just a few decades previously. Immigrants flooding into the United States inflated the urban population from six million in 1860 to forty-two million in 1910.

As a group, early Pentecostals were ferociously committed to converting others, both near and far. They believed that God was at work in a special way, and they wanted to tell others about it. Pentecostal converts with little formal training became overseas missionaries by buying one-way tickets to every corner of the globe, convinced that God would take care of the details once they arrived at their destinations. Some of these "one-way ticket" missionaries brought Pentecostalism to Brazil.

Fewer than five years after Seymour opened the doors at Azusa, two Swedish immigrants, Daniel Berg and Gunnar Vingren, heard a voice repeating the word "Para ... Para ... Para" over and over during a group prayer session in Indiana. No one in the prayer group had heard of such a place, but they were certain it was a message from God. Convinced they were not looking for a city in Indiana, they took a trip to the Chicago Public Library and scoured world maps until they found the Brazilian state of Pará tucked into the country's northeast corner, situated at the mouth of the Amazon. Seeing Pará on the map was all the convincing they needed. Undeterred by the lack of Portuguese fluency, financial support, or Brazilian connections, the two men purchased one-way tickets and boarded a steamship in New York. They landed in Pará's capital city, Belém, on November 19, 1910, and began to spread the Pentecostal message.

Again, these were not well-educated movers and shakers; rather, they were exactly the types of people who advanced the movement. Berg was a steelworker, and though Vingren had taken courses at a Swedish-speaking seminary in Chicago, he was just twenty-one years old when he landed in Brazil. The two men rented space in the basement of a Baptist church in Belém, and by June 1911 the first Brazilian Pentecostal, Celina Alburquerque, started speaking in tongues. The Swedish American missionaries were ecstatic with their early success, but the Baptist church that hosted the group had a very different reaction to the glossolalia coming from the church basement. They expelled the group. This small group of castouts continued to meet and eventually became the seed from which sprouted the Assemblies of God denomination in Brazil.

The same year that Berg and Vingren started their church in Belém, an Italian immigrant, Luigi Francescon, began preaching a spirit-infused Christianity to the growing number of Italian immigrants in São Paulo. Francescon was a product of the Azusa Street Revival and was briefly mentored by William Durham. Like the gathering of

Pentecostals in Belém, Francescon and his group of Italian immigrants were thrown out of their host church shortly after they began speaking in tongues. Resistance from the Catholic Church was expected, but the established Protestant churches were also not comfortable partnering with this version of Christianity. Just like his counterparts in Belém, Francescon began a new denomination, the Christian Congregation (Congregação Cristã).

The first wave of Brazilian Pentecostalism's growth occurred through these two denominations, the Assemblies of God and Congregação Cristã. Paul Freston (1994) described Brazilian Pentecostalism as a "national, popular, and rapidly expanding phenomenon" (537). Though the missionaries who brought this faith to Brazil had been European immigrants coming from the United States, the foreign influence in Pentecostalism was short-lived as Brazilian leaders quickly rose to the top of denominations. By the 1930s, the Assemblies of God denomination planted by the Swedes was led entirely by Brazilians, and the last foreign-based denomination to make a substantial impact on Brazil's Pentecostal population was the Four Square Church in the 1950s.

Pentecostal growth in Brazil has been extraordinary. In 1900, there was simply no such thing as a Brazilian Pentecostal, but by 1949 there were over 200,000 Pentecostals in Brazil (Chesnut 1997). The burgeoning faith experienced another wave of growth that coincided with the mass urbanization process Brazil experienced in the 1950s and early 1960s. Many of the migrants pouring into Brazilian cities eagerly embraced the new movement. A third wave of Pentecostal growth occurred in the 1980s and 1990s. This most recent efflorescence occurred at the same time and in the same places as the birth and growth of narco-gangs in Rio de Janeiro (Freston 1994).

One of the features common to all three waves of Pentecostal growth in Brazil has been an ability to incorporate the local culture's DNA into the faith. In a recent interview, Andrew Chesnut was asked why this version of Christianity has grown so quickly in Latin America. He responded by saying,

Pentecostalism has very successfully absorbed Latin American culture. So, for example, the music that you hear in Pentecostal churches has the same rhythms that people enjoy outside of church. In fact, in only a century, Pentecostalism has become indigenous, or "Latin Americanized," to a greater extent than Roman Catholicism has in its four centuries in Latin America. And the Pentecostal preachers tend to sound more like their congregants. They are often unlettered and they speak to their flock in the same way that people in Latin American speak to each other. They also tend to look like their congregants. So in Guatemala, many preachers are Mayan, and in Brazil they are Afro-Brazilian. By contrast, in the Catholic Church, most priests are part of the elite. They are either white or mestizo and many are actually from Europe. (Chesnut 2014)

Brazilian Pentecostalism didn't depend on direction from Rome—or from Los Angeles, for that matter—and leaders were not imported but rather emerged from within the congregations. Pentecostal churches stood in stark contrast to the Catholic Church and other powerful institutions that privileged well-educated elites. Recently Pentecostalism has made inroads into the Brazilian middle class, and to a lesser extent national politics, but throughout the history of the faith's presence in Brazil it has been a movement that looks and sounds like the masses.

WHY SO FAR SO FAST?

The dramatic growth and social impact of Pentecostalism in Latin America have not been lost on social scientists. Sociologists, anthropologists, political scientists, and historians started to study the movement in the late 1960s. Practicing Pentecostals tend to explain the growth of the religion by pointing to unseen spiritual forces, but according to David Smilde (2007) "the dominant social scientific interpretation is that Latin American Evangelicalism [Pentecostalism] is a religion orientated toward those experiencing sustained life problems, or 'dis-ease'" (55), and "conversion to Pentecostalism serves as a form of cultural agency through which they can gain control over aspects of their personal and social contexts" (5). In other words, Pentecostalism offers a unique set of tools that allows adherents to confront life crises like anomie, physical illness, violence, substance addiction, marital strife, a stigmatized identity, and financial instability.

Emilio Willems (1967) conducted the first anthropological research on Pentecostals in Latin America by studying groups in both Brazil and Chile. Willems conducted his fieldwork as each country was still adjusting to decades of industrialization, modernization, and urbanization. The social structures of these countries were in flux as migrants poured from the countryside into Brazilian *favelas* and Chile's urban *villas*. Many urban migrants had traveled to cities by themselves, leaving family and friends behind, which meant they were isolated, lonely, and searching for community. Willems argued that Pentecostal churches helped to ease the emotional burden by providing a family-like atmosphere during and after services as well as a tightly knit group of people who shared their lives. Though 1960s Pentecostalism in Latin America was full of rules dictating significant parts of adherents' daily lives, Willems argued that the faith was nonetheless a radically disruptive force as it challenged the existing social structure by placing peasants and people with no social ties to the middle and upper classes in leadership positions.

Other scholars understood Pentecostalism's success in Latin America as a product of its ability to meet people's material and emotional needs. Cecilia Loreto Mariz (1994) studied Pentecostalism in Brazil's poorest region, the arid Northeast, and in her analysis she framed the faith as a mechanism that enabled Pentecostals to understand and cope with the chronic poverty plaguing the region. Since Pentecostals were a distinct minority in the predominantly Catholic society of northeastern Brazil, Mariz argued that their minority status created strong in-group ties among the faithful that nurtured networks to help the poor to survive difficult conditions. This strong identity fortified them in the face of persecution from the broader culture, but it also provided a valuable safety net that helped them cope with poverty.

Like Willems, Mariz focused on intra-faith relationships: "Pentecostalism creates an alternative network of support. For most Pentecostals, this informational network is more helpful for their material survival than the institutional church itself" (93). According to Mariz, Pentecostals confronted poverty by creating relational networks among fellow church members. The Pentecostals in Mariz's study did not become rich, but they endured poverty better than they would have otherwise.

When the Swedish American missionaries Berg and Vingren arrived in Belém on the steamship, they landed in a city that Chesnut (1997) described as an "incubator for disease" (27). Daniel Berg wrote, "It was wrenching to see the poor classes, treated so harshly in life, laden with the added burden of sickness. Some who had lost family members to illness came to visit us in our small room, seeking comfort in the word of God" (Chesnut 1997, 28). In the mid-1990s Chesnut studied Pentecostalism in Belém, but he was not convinced that poverty alone could explain the eighty-plus years of Pentecostal history in the city. Chesnut relied on historical sources and ninety in-depth interviews with practicing Pentecostals in Belém's *baixadas* (the local term used to describe *favelas*) to argue that the faith's ability to respond to health problems that were consequences of poverty also contributed to its growth. Most of the interviewees in Chesnut's study converted either during or after a health emergency, and through historical sources he convincingly argued that these sorts of conversions had been a key component of Pentecostal growth in Belém since the faith arrived in 1910.

Unlike missionaries from other Christian denominations, the Pentecostals did not build hospitals or healthcare facilities; instead they confronted individuals' health crises in two ways. First, the faith promised unmediated access to the supernatural, specifically to miraculous healing, to people with scarce access to formal healthcare. In Chesnut's study, nearly 90 percent of interviewees reported being cured by Jesus or the Holy Spirit, nearly double the number who reported speaking in tongues (80).

Determining whether respondents were *actually* healed through supernatural intervention is not possible through social scientific research methods, but the fact that so many of Belém's Pentecostals experienced what they interpreted as a faith healing provides a powerful foundation for the argument that poverty by itself is not a sufficient explanation of Pentecostal growth.

The other way Pentecostalism addressed disease among Belém's poor was to "immunize" them from what Chesnut refers to as the pathogens of poverty:

> The crente [believer] still inhabits an impoverished world but now, through an ascetic lifestyle, has the power to resist many of the contagions spawned by poverty. Conversion to Pentecostalism is no panacea for the multiple viruses caused by material deprivation, but it does immunize its followers against some of poverty's more pernicious strains. (83)

Pentecostalism is a strict religion. It prescribes how a believer should allocate his or her resources and spend free time, and it prohibits behaviors like drinking, sexual promiscuity, and drug use. Whether the faith healings were as frequent as reported by Chesnut's respondents, or whether they even occurred all, is not the point of his argument. The behavioral guidelines set by the faith could effectively mitigate behaviors that were harmful to a believer's health and finances in impoverished families that had few resources to respond to additional adversities. For this reason, the Pentecostal lifestyle can be understood as a preventative healthcare strategy.

Pentecostalism has resonated not only with Latin America's marginalized, but with the region's stigmatized as well. In research that profoundly influenced this book, Robert Brenneman (2011) studied the intersection of two of the most consequential social phenomena to emerge in Central America over the last two decades: transnational street gangs and heavily Pentecostal Christianity. Both social phenomena have had deeply consequential impacts on society in Guatemala, El Salvador, and Honduras, and Brenneman's work examines how some members have transitioned out of Mara Salvatrucha and other infamous Central American gangs and attempted to create new lives for themselves in the gritty *barrios* of the "Northern Triangle" by converting to Pentecostalism.

Central American gang members are feared by nearly everyone in the region. Media portrayals of heavily tattooed young men armed to the teeth are framed by the region's staggering crime and homicide rates to make this group the most stigmatized in Central American society. Most governments in the region have engaged these groups with violence and have encouraged people to blame the gangs for nearly all of Central America's social problems. The gangs are Central America's killable people.

Until relatively recently, Guatemala, Honduras, and El Salvador were thoroughly Catholic nations. After periods of Protestant growth and stagnation starting in the 1960s, the region experienced an evangelical "boom" in the 1990s that was largely led by local religious leaders and Central American–based evangelistic campaigns. Today, nearly one-third of all Central Americans in the Northern Triangle describe themselves as Protestants. Brenneman introduced the term "barrio evangelicalism" to describe the type of Christianity practiced by the ex-gang members in his study, whom he defines as "theologically conservative, liturgically Pentecostal, locally oriented congregations of the neighborhood or 'barrio'" (57). This is the same faith I describe as Pentecostalism in this book.

One of the requirements to join a gang is agreeing to be a member "hasta la morgue." Still, the gangs recognize a member's converting to Pentecostalism as a legitimate way to say *adios* to the gang, and they pardon the defectors as long as they publicly embrace the rigid and demanding faith. By interviewing more than sixty ex-gang members, Brenneman reveals an interesting interplay between a convert's ability to avoid the "morgue rule" and his reported life-changing contact with an unseen supernatural force. It would be easy to conceptualize these conversions as simply premeditated, rational choices by gang members who were tired of gang life and wanted to opt for the only exit available, but it is clear that the decision to become a *hermano* is considerably more complex. Many of the interviewees report an intense, emotional experience; additionally, many admit to breaking down and publicly weeping during conversion (a practice that runs counter to the *machismo* culture of Central America).

The respect shown to Pentecostals by the Central American gangs mirrors the attitudes toward Pentecostal movements shared by residents of the *favelas* of Rio. My purpose in this book is to move this investigation forward by examining how the complex set of benefits that Pentecostalism affords Rio's most marginalized communities—dark-skinned prison inmates from the city's *favelas*—is captured in the notion of dignity. Instead of framing Pentecostalism simply as a way to cope with or adapt to a difficult situation, I focus on how it offers dignity to people who have been systemically oppressed—treated without dignity—by the surrounding society. In this context Pentecostalism offers the believer a new identity and, importantly, a set of spiritual practices that allows him or her to become someone new. The convert may not become rich or rise in social class, but Pentecostalism offers a new paradigm on which to base one's self-worth.

PENTECOSTALISM IN RIO DE JANEIRO

Pentecostalism experienced rapid growth in Rio's *favelas* in the late 1990s. Social scientists, including those with Marxist perspectives, can debate which theoretical lens best explains the proliferation of Pentecostalism in the city's *favelas* over the last twenty years, but the presence of the movement in low-income neighborhoods is not up for debate.

I spoke about the religious landscape in Rio de Janeiro with Francisco, an ex-inmate who had converted to Pentecostalism in prison. I first met Francisco outside of the entrance to Salgado Jail while he was dressed in a dusty suit two sizes too big and praying with his hands raised in the air as he was preparing to enter the jail. Francisco had spent time in half a dozen prisons and jails in Rio de Janeiro, including seven months in Salgado, before his conversion.

When he visited the jail to preach and pray with the inmates he always started his sermon by pointing to the patch of concrete on the cell floor where he used to sleep. Francisco wanted the men to understand that he had known the same humiliation and suffering that they were experiencing.

Out of prison for more than five years, Francisco lived with his wife and children in a poor neighborhood on the outskirts of Rio. I visited him at his home one afternoon, and while we sat on his steps, I asked him how many churches were within walking distance of his house. He was a member of a nearby Assemblies of God congregation and to respond to my question he stood up on the stairs and started to point to the churches as he counted them off:

> Okay, there is one at the front, two with mine [the Assemblies of God denomination], three with the God is Power. Then if you go up from the God Is Power there is another four or five with the community, six with another Assemblies of God, and seven with the God Is Love. So there are seven Pentecostal churches and one traditional Baptist church.

Francisco's neighborhood was full of Pentecostal churches, as were most poor neighborhoods in Rio. In fact, the sheer number of Pentecostal churches is now one of the defining features of Rio's low-income neighborhoods. Most if not all of Rio's favelas are peppered with the signs of storefront churches as well as a surprising number of large Pentecostal temples. In the *favela* controlled by the Comando Vermelho that I described in the previous chapter, I asked the deacon of an Assemblies of God church the same question I asked Francisco: "How many Pentecostal churches are in this neighborhood?"

He told me that in the cluster of favelas where we stood, there were more than eighty thousand residents and "about ninety Pentecostal churches here and a couple of Catholic churches, but no Macumba centers."[4] Gangs like the Comando Vermelho are not the only groups that have grown in the unique conditions found in the *favelas* and other poor neighborhoods in Rio de Janeiro—Pentecostalism has flourished as well.

GANGS AND PENTECOSTALS SHARING
THE SPACE

Given the history of Pentecostal growth at the economic margins, it should come as no surprise that the faith does well in the *favelas*. What may be surprising is the nature of the relationship between the gang and the church. At first glance, these two groups would appear to be natural rivals because dual membership in the organizations is not permitted. The Pentecostals preach submission to God, temperance, and interaction with the Holy Spirit, while the gangs offer access to a more tangible trinity: money, sex, and power. But surprisingly, the relationship between the church and the gang is not defined by animosity. Pentecostal church members are active in gang-controlled areas, and much of their work is indirectly or sometimes directly supported by narco-gangs.

I asked Elizeu dos Santos, the pastor of the Way of the Just Church, an Assemblies of God congregation on the outskirts of Rio, to explain how this counterintuitive relationship plays out in his community. He gave me the following example:

> I had a project inside a community, inside a *favela*, and on the side of
> the community center there was an open-air drug market. Every time
> I went there, they transferred the *boca de fumo* to a different place.
> They [the gang] didn't want to endanger the people who were coming
> to the worship service. They don't let people smoke, snort cocaine close
> to us, nobody. Sometimes when we come and they are smoking drugs,
> they hide it. You can smell it, but they are like "hey, the pastor is here;
> hide that."

I saw this sort of interplay between the gang and the church repeatedly. The gang would alter its drug distribution strategy during a church program or worship service, recognizing that drug sales were disrespectful to the Pentecostals. Even though it may have hurt business on that day, the gang consistently made accommodations for Pentecostal groups to work with youth, hold street revivals, or do service projects like hand out food and provide basic medical care to the people living in *Cracolandia* (Crackland). The gang's accommodations were consistent but always temporary.

Pastor Elizeu told me that at times, specifically during a street revival, the gang would help his church set up the chairs and would even let the church borrow the sound system that the gang used to host its funk parties:

> They [gang members] have tremendous respect for us. They actually help us a lot. When we go inside a *favela*, they open a space for us in the neighborhood. They carry in chairs on their head, or they give a soda or sandwich for everyone there. The drug traffickers tell me, "Hey, pastor, whatever you need, it will be there." They bring a sound system, a complete sound system, and we do our work. They really care for us. If there is drug use, they stop it because "the brothers are here."

In some neighborhoods the Comando Vermelho has done more than just modify drug-distribution points and help set up chairs and speakers—members have used their influence to manipulate religious choice in their neighborhoods to favor Pentecostalism. When a deacon from the Assemblies of God told me that in the cluster of *favelas* where we stood there were no Macumba centers, I followed up with a question about the absence of Macumba centers. He told me that the neighborhood's religious marketplace was not entirely open. There may have been demand for Macumba centers, but the Comando Vermelho prohibited the religious practice. Like many Pentecostals, CV views Macumba as Pentecostalists' enemy number one, because Macumba and Pentecostalism are thought to have roots in opposite sides of the spiritual realm. The gang members, in a sign of support and respect toward the Pentecostals (and in the hope of reducing their chances of being on the receiving end of a curse) prohibited the practice of Macumba in the neighborhoods they controlled.

The mutually respectful interactions I witnessed between the narco-gangs and the Pentecostals begs a simple question: Why? If the two organizations are competing for members from the same neighborhoods and dual membership is not an option, why is there not more animosity or apparent competition between the two groups? Not only are they competing for the same members, but the Pentecostals also actively encourage people to leave gangs. From the gang's perspective, doesn't this relationship threaten the gang's powerful role in the *favelas*?

During the fieldwork, I visited many neighborhoods that had a strong gang presence. In all of them, Pentecostalism was the principal faith. A pastor in one of these neighborhoods told me, "The majority of criminals in Rio are children of Pentecostals." The pastor was not implying that being raised in a Pentecostal home led to criminal activity or gang affiliation but rather he illuminated one of the key reasons that Pentecostalism is respected by the gangs. Gang members, more so than almost any other group in Rio de Janeiro, are raised in places where Pentecostalism is the dominant faith.

Many gang members have parents, aunts, cousins, and siblings who are active in Pentecostal churches. The social and class differences that exist between gang members and other institutions—the government, politics, universities, middle-class employment, for example—do not exist between the gangs and the Pentecostals in poor neighborhoods. And conversely, many pastors and active Pentecostal church leaders were once gang members themselves or have family members currently in the gang. Because of these shared life experiences, Pentecostals treat gang members differently than how the rest of the city treats gangs. Because many church leaders are born in the same *favelas* as the gang members, their words have a weight and authenticity that an outsider's words may not hold.

There are few atheists in the ranks of Rio's gangs or inside *favela* houses. The cultural belief that God exists and is active in the world saturates this part of the city, including the gangs. Evidence of belief in a generically Christian God appears in the gang's material culture.

Though I don't have an exact count, I am certain that the phrase most frequently tattooed on the forearms and backs of Comando Vermelho members was "Deus é Fiel" (God is faithful). Music, specifically "funk" music, is an important part of gang culture. Funk lyrics praise the gang, promote its values, and frequently weave references to the supernatural into songs that glorify violence, promiscuous sexual activity, and devotion to the gang. For example, an underground funk song popular with the Comando Vermelho was "F em Deus," by MC Duduzinho (2009). The first verse and chorus are as follows:

> Change [the ammo clip], shoot, boom!
> Eject the clip.
> Don't be afraid, the enemy is already
>   coming.
> The time is coming
> Before heading out to another war.
> I said a prayer to God
> That he will protect us on this important mission.
>
> Faith in God! I am Comando Vermelho until I die.
> More faith in God. Whoever agrees flash the sign!
>   (my translation)

I spoke with many inmates who told me that they used to pray immediately before they committed an armed assault or invaded a rival gang's neighborhood. This culturally held belief among gang members that a supernatural being exists and is active in the world is not unique to Rio. During Robert Brenneman's (2011) fieldwork in Central America (2011), a gang leader told him why the leader's gang releases people from their gang obligations if they convert and become practicing Pentecostals: "Okay. You know that nobody messes with Curly [El Colocho, meaning God]. Not with Curly not with the barrio [gang]" (159).

Because there are not many atheists in Rio's gangs, the theological leap they make when they convert to Pentecostalism may not be as large as it may first appear. The question most of them face is not whether God exists, but whether they will submit their lives, identity, and actions to God in the manner prescribed in Pentecostal theology.

Though Pentecostals chip away at the gangs by recruiting hundreds of young men away from their ranks each year, they do not threaten the organization's position of dominance in the *favelas*. Church leaders may publicly pray that the drug-distribution points will close down, but they do not stage protests, threaten the gang, or call on government authorities to remove them. I have never heard of a Pentecostal campaign to rid their neighborhood of a particular gang, nor speak out loud against a specific gang leader. If the Pentecostals in Rio's gang-controlled neighborhoods led organized campaigns to expel the gangs from their neighborhoods, the relationship between the two organizations would likely look much different. It would also look very different if the Pentecostals cooperated with the police.

RESPECT THE PASTOR

In the last chapter I described my first visit to a Comando Vermelho–controlled neighborhood in the company of a pastor, an Assemblies of God deacon and a recently converted Pentecostal who had recently ended a multiyear crack cocaine addiction. I ended the vignette with the four of us waiting to meet with the Comando Vermelho boss. After waiting fifteen minutes we were summoned by an armed teenager who told us that the CV leader was ready to speak to us. The pastor had called for the meeting because the gang decided to shut down *Cracolandia*, the open-air crack market that had been operating thirty yards from the table where they sold marijuana and powder cocaine. The number of crack users had dropped from a few hundred to a few dozen since the CV announced that crack sales would stop, and the remaining users smoked the small, pale-yellow rocks under printed signs that read "THE SALE OF CRACK WILL SOON BE PROHIBITED HERE."

The CV leader arrived with a semiautomatic pistol tucked into his shorts, a thick Rolex on one wrist, a two-inch-wide gold bracelet on the other, and chunky gold rings on three of his fingers. Two bodyguards, who were also dripping in gold, accompanied the CV leader everywhere he went. We all shook hands, and the pastor started the conversation by telling them that God was pleased with their decision to stop selling crack because the drug destroys individuals and families.

The gang leader shrugged in agreement and continued to listen to the pastor as he told the gang members how he hoped God would continue his work in the community and eventually end the "rest of this," pointing to the three sofas full of teenagers and the open-air drug buffet.

Though the pastor made it clear that the drug business was not a neutral activity in God's eyes, he did not vilify the gang members. He did not accuse them of anything immoral or imply that they were the root of the problems facing the neighborhood and city (a wise move, considering all three men were heavily armed). I could sense that the men lowered their emotional defenses in response to the firm but respectful way the pastor spoke with them. He brought a positive message, telling them that God was pleased with their decision to stop selling crack, as opposed to saying God was displeased with them selling drugs.

Building on the moment, the pastor then asked if he could pray with the three men. The gang leader nodded in consent, and the pastor, deacon, and former crack user placed their hands on the men's shoulders and began to pray. Though the gang members were not Pentecostals, when the pastor started to pray, all three immediately bowed their heads, closed their eyes, and accepted the prayers, as well as the touch of the other men. The pastor prayed that God would protect these three men and thanked God for their decision to stop the sale of crack cocaine in the space they controlled. He prayed for blessings and peace in the neighborhood, which had been one of Rio's most violent over the last decade, and ended by thanking God for the men's lives.

In stark contrast to how much of the city talks about and treats gang members, the pastor prayed as if the gang members' lives had value. He affirmed their dignity even though they all were carrying weapons and the leader held a sack of drug money in his hands. The pastor's interaction with the men was radically different from the interactions these men have with the police, government officials, the media, and the rest of society. The pastor directly spoke against the gang's drug business and indirectly against their control of their neighborhood, but not against the gang members as people. In short, he treated them with dignity. I argue that this sort of interaction is one of the primary reasons that Pentecostals are treated with respect in these areas.

There were no tears from the gang members, no signs of remorse, no confessions, and no promises to change their affiliation with the Comando Vermelho. But after the final amen the gang members thanked us for coming and we all hugged each other. As we said our farewells, the pastor asked if he could take some photographs of the nearly empty *Cracolandia* area to show that progress was being made in this neighborhood. Our group followed the pastor down the train tracks as he snapped photos that he would later send to the local newspaper.

The sun had set, so after a few hundred yards we were out of the gang leader's sight. The flash from the pastor's camera attracted unwanted attention, and we were soon accosted by a group of young men coming from the other direction. They barked orders at our group and demanded that the pastor turn over his camera. This new group of CV members was also armed and not joking around, so I was uneasy when the deacon and the other man in our group started to yell, "This is a pastor—you can't talk to him like that!" As tempers flared, I froze and could hear my heart beating inside my chest.

Finally, one of the gang members called his boss on his cellphone, whom we had just met. Thankfully while the young man spoke to his boss, the tone of his voice changed dramatically. When he ended the call, he apologized profusely and asked us to forgive the rude treatment. The tension and aggression in the air immediately dissipated and then, for the second time in twenty minutes, we were once again hugging and saying goodbye to a small group of CV members. As one of the young men gave me a quick embrace and apologized, I felt the butt of his weapon press against the side of my stomach and was grateful for cell phones.

Not all Pentecostal and gang interactions are as cooperative as the ones I observed firsthand or heard about in the interviews I conducted. In 2009, Pastor Odilon Calixto da Cunha arrived in the Vigário Geral *favela* in Rio de Janeiro from the neighboring state of Minas Gerais to pastor a Deus é Amor (God Is Love) Pentecostal church. Rio can be a difficult place for Brazilians from other regions to gain acceptance because of cultural differences and regional rivalries, but the pastor did not help his cause when he refused to accept stolen food from the back of a truck hijacked by the Pure Third Comando, the gang that controlled Vigário Geral.

The relationship between the pastor and the gang worsened when gang members arrived at his house days later with a colleague who had just been shot. Pastor Odilon told them that his car was broken and he could not take the wounded man to the hospital. Soon after, the gang's leader called the pastor to a face-to-face meeting and accused him of being a police informant. The meeting didn't end well, and the next day, three armed gang members invaded the pastor's house and physically removed the pastor and his family, literally throwing them into the street.

On November 23, 2009, Pastor Odilon told the O Dia newspaper, "I know I shouldn't be so angry, but when my youngest, a two-year-old, was lying on the sidewalk, cold and hugging me, I could not want anything other than that they all be arrested and pay for the humiliation that they put us through. It was very cowardly to send my wife and children out of the house with only the clothes on their backs, not even letting them eat the food that was on the stove. I want them to suffer."

The nature of the relationship between the gang and the church is not uniform in the city and depends on the personalities and leadership styles of the pastors and gang leaders who operate in a given neighborhood. Like any relationship, there are a number of variables at work. Did the pastor just arrive? Do other pastors in the neighborhood have a clandestine relationship with the gang members or are at least willing to cooperate with them? Is the gang leader particularly surly?

Another set of problems arises when the relationship between the pastor and gang goes *too* well. How close can a pastor get to the gang before he compromises his principles and puts himself and his ministry at risk? Though working with gang leaders is necessary to do nearly any sort of ministry in gang-controlled neighborhoods, this working relationship can put pastors in precarious situations.

I accompanied a pastor when he visited Niko, the Comando Vermelho leader who was in the CV safe house during the invasion of the Complexo de Alemão. The pastor had recently developed a relationship with Niko in order to get his permission to start an educational program for children in the neighborhood and to try to persuade Niko to give his life to God. Shortly after we arrived in the neighborhood, Niko, with a semiautomatic pistol on his hip, approached us on a motorcycle worth tens of thousands of dollars. He had one of his subordinates bring us to an outdoor table and chairs while he stashed his gun so he wouldn't be showing disrespect to the pastor. Unarmed, Niko spoke with us for half an hour until his lunch was ready, then he invited us to continue the conversation in his living room while he ate.

The interior of Niko's apartment, located in a very poor *favela*, looked nothing like his neighbors' homes. It was outfitted with over-stuffed furniture that surrounded a wall-mounted flat-screen television, and it was decorated with an impressive display of luxury liquor bottles lit by neon lights. The pastor invited me to join him so he wouldn't be alone with Niko, and I mostly listened as the two men spoke frankly about police activity in the neighborhood and the warrant out for Niko's arrest. Niko seemed to enjoy the conversation and spoke to the pastor as a peer, but as we said goodbye he let the pastor know that he had no intention of converting to Pentecostalism or turning himself in to the authorities.

Given the realities of the gangs' presence in Rio's low-income neighborhoods, pastors wade into morally murky waters when they interact with people like Niko. I do not want to ignore the social forces that gave rise to the drug trade, but there is no doubt that gang leaders are directly responsible for tremendous pain and destruction in the lives of individuals and the surrounding community. This moral gray area was cast into a harsh light when the pastor and I left Niko's apartment and went on a "tour" of the neighborhood accompanied by a gang-affiliated community leader. At the pastor's request we visited the *Cracolandia* under Niko's direct control. When we arrived there were over a dozen people living in plastic tents and sleeping on torn mattresses on the ground in a secluded area next to the train tracks. The area was littered with thousands of small empty plastic crack bags that were printed with the logo of Niko's gang.

The pastor approached two young women who were living there and asked if they would tell us their stories. Both said that they were there because they were "slaves" to crack. One of the women started what had become a two-year crack addiction after a fire destroyed her home and killed her mother and only child. Homeless, alone, and profoundly depressed, she said she started to smoke the drug. The other young woman first smoked crack while she was in jail, and for the last three years she had become involved in prostitution in order to support her habit.

The pastor and I sat in shocked silence as she told us in detail about what the johns who came to *Cracolandia* would do to her. They were not just looking to use someone for sex—they could find those services almost anywhere—but to find someone they could violently abuse. They knew they could find the city's most vulnerable, least protected sex workers in that place.

The pastor and I were emotionally shaken by the women's stories and by the tears that fell from their vacant eyes and streamed down their emaciated cheeks. These women put a face to the consequences of Niko's business, and they served as a painful reminder that his gangster-chic apartment was funded in part by their addiction. Seeing Niko through the lens of *Cracolandia* put his role in the drug trade into a different perspective because he was profiting from the hellish situation we saw in front of us. I felt different about just having sat on his sofa.

As we left the neighborhood that afternoon, the pastor and I spoke with each other about the day. Each of us was unsettled by what we had seen, and the pastor started to wonder aloud about how many lives Niko had helped to destroy, indirectly through his crack business and directly by his own hands. How many people had he murdered in his rise to power? Even though the pastor sought out Niko to talk about opening a children's education program, did he cross a line by accepting Niko's hospitality?

Another concerning aspect of our visit was the community members' perception of the pastor. We started our conversation with Niko in a very public place, and certainly everyone in the surrounding neighborhood knew that the two of us went into Niko's home. What sort of message did that send to the rest of the community? Was the pastor condoning Niko's behavior? If I lived in the neighborhood, and Niko or a member of his gang had killed a member of my family, how would I feel if I saw the pastor enter Niko's house and sit in his living room?

Two weeks after our conversation, I passed by a newspaper stand close to my apartment and did a literal double take. Photos of Niko's apartment were all over the front page of one of Rio's daily newspapers. The previous day, police had raided his house, and though Niko had escaped the raid, photos of his place were now selling newspapers.

When I saw the sofa where I had sat prominently featured on the front page, I immediately thought, "What if the raid had happened while we were there?" Assuming that we would not have been injured or worse, who knows what would have happened to me? The pastor would have likely been arrested, and at best his reputation would have taken a serious hit. For pastors, meeting with people like Niko may be necessary to minister outside of the four walls of the church, but that can also be a risky endeavor.

A WORLD OF AZUSA STREETS

The Pentecostalism now practiced in Rio's *favelas* is the fruit of a religious movement that started just over one hundred years ago in a converted horse stable on the edge of downtown Los Angeles. From the first services held at Azusa Street to the thousands of Pentecostal communities in twenty-first-century Rio de Janeiro, Pentecostalism is a faith that has thrived on the margins of society. Starting with William Seymour, global Pentecostalism has been a religious movement primarily led by the poor, immigrants, racial minorities, and those stigmatized by the larger society.

One reason that Pentecostalism has flourished in Latin America's harshest urban environments is its ability to incorporate local culture into the religious practice and to empower leadership that is indigenous to the community. The music in the churches has the same beat as the music in the streets, and pastors preach in the same vernacular used in conversations at the bus stop, in corner cafés, and in the local markets. Pastors and Pentecostal leaders can rise from the congregations without having to go through seminaries or other educational institutions that are available to the middle and upper classes but largely closed to others.

Though Brazil is the world's largest Catholic country, and Rio de Janeiro is still a predominantly Catholic city, in poor neighborhoods like the Complexo de Alemão Pentecostalism is the dominant faith. In Rio de Janeiro, that also means that thousands of Pentecostal churches operate in neighborhoods that are controlled by narco-gangs.

In general, Pentecostals in Rio treat active gang members differently than the rest of society treats them, and the nature of the interactions I witnessed between Pentecostals and gang members in Rio was consistent. The pastors and church members told the gang members that their lives had value and that God offered something better for them than the life that the gang could provide. They rarely acknowledged the larger social factors that may have pushed gang members into that world, but unlike the police and much of the rest of Rio's residents, Pentecostals do not regard the gang members as if they were killable people. In turn, the gangs treat Pentecostals, especially pastors, with respect.

Evidence of this relationship can be observed when the gang members pack up their tables full of narcotics and move it to a different part of the neighborhood when the Pentecostals come to hold a street revival or provide some sort of social service. In some of Rio's neighborhoods, the gang actively intervenes in the religious marketplace and restricts the practice of religious movements that are perceived as rivals to Pentecostalism. Because both institutions are strongest in the same parts of the city, pastors and gang leaders often have symbiotic relationships. Still, pastors have to be careful about aligning themselves too closely with the gangs who are involved in activities that their faith prohibits. For their part, gang leaders treat the churches with respect, but they still do whatever it takes to maintain their control over the neighborhood.

Religious identification surveys consistently show that Pentecostal Christianity is the future of global Christianity. The faith has thrived among the urban poor. As the world's urban population steadily increases in the developing world, it appears as if Pentecostalism's presence, like in Rio de Janeiro, will be even more important in twenty years than it is today.

For the purposes of this book, Rio's prisons are cultural extensions of the *favelas*. Pentecostalism's success in the city's poor neighborhoods and the nature of the relationship between the Pentecostal movements and the gangs are crucial to understanding how religion is practiced inside of prison. The following chapters explore this relationship in much greater depth.

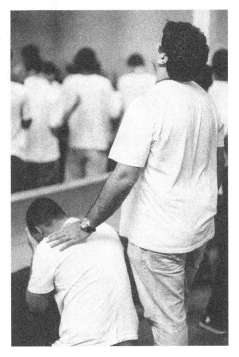

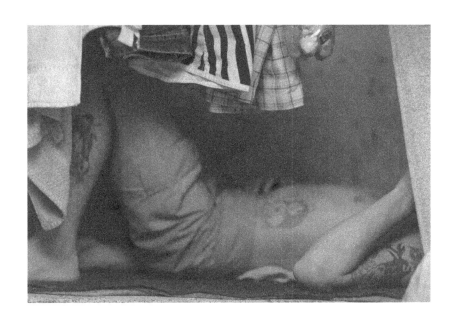

CHAPTER 4

A GANG
OF PENTECOSTALS

RELIGIOUS PRACTICE BEHIND BARS
IN RIO DE JANEIRO

At exactly six o'clock the Comando Vermelho's *grito de guerra* (war cry) rang out from the cells in Salgado's south wing, started by the throaty shout from a single detainee. The lone voice was immediately answered by the four hundred inmates living in the gang-controlled cells, and everyone else throughout the facility stopped what they were doing and stood silent when the gang's call-and-response ritual began. The war cry built to a crescendo, then ended with the repetition of the powerful final phrase five times: "Comando ... Vermelho, Comando ... Vermelho, Comando ... Vermelho, Comando ... Vermelho, Comando ... Vermelho."

A somber hush fell over the building, and in the silence that followed I asked an inmate standing next to me what I had just heard. He responded, "It's their war cry. They do this every day and always at six o'clock." The daily ritual reminds both the inmates and the guards that Rio de Janeiro's most powerful gang, the Comando Vermelho (Red Command), controls the south wing of the jail.

But that wasn't the first *grito de guerra* I had heard that day. Fewer than thirty minutes earlier, on the other side of the facility, the members of the Heroes for Christ Prison Church performed a strikingly similar ritual. After the ninety-minute worship service, the pastor of Heroes for Christ, an inmate himself, yelled at the top of his lungs, "By what are we saved?" Then the thirty participants answered, "By the blood of Christ!"

The pastor continued, this time with more intensity, "If he is your shepherd?" The inmates responded, matching the pastor's heightened passion: "Then we will lack nothing!" The inmate pastor continued leading the call and response, pacing through his incarcerated congregation to make his final, most dramatic declaration: "Church, together with all the inmates here, with tremendous faith, give us Lord Jesus . . ." and all of the men let loose with everything they had—"FREEDOM!!!"

In Rio de Janeiro, autonomous, inmate-led prison churches like the Heroes for Christ Prison Church are the heart of Pentecostal practice behind bars. "The church is ours. It belongs to those of us on the inside," Cristiano, a Salgado inmate and the leader of the church's war cry, told me. "Some churches from the outside visit, but there isn't formal sponsorship. We are not a legal entity. . . . It is a community church."

Cristiano's church is a community church in the most literal sense. Every church member comes from the immediate community—the prison population. Obviously, prison churches operate in a very different social milieu than other Pentecostal churches. Though the theology of the prison churches is similar to Pentecostal churches on the street, the organizational structure and daily operations of the churches are substantially different from other forms of Pentecostalism.

One reason these churches have flourished inside prisons is demographics. Inmates in Rio's men's prisons are disproportionately young, poor, and darker-skinned when compared to the rest of the city's residents. That means that the prison population comprises the same sociodemographic category as the other urban spaces in Rio where Pentecostalism has been most successful.

We might expect that the patterns of religious affiliation in prison would reflect that of the neighborhoods where the prisoners come from. But the Pentecostal prison churches are more than just a continuation of the faith's success among Rio's urban poor. The Pentecostalism practiced inside of Rio's prisons, Prison Pentecostalism, is profoundly shaped by the prison context.

In this chapter, I will introduce Prison Pentecostalism by comparing the structure and role of the Pentecostal churches inside of prison to the structure and role of prison gangs. I will not argue that the Pentecostal prison churches are really just gangs that have "found religion," or that the gangs are "churches of violence." Rather, I will show that understanding Prison Pentecostalism's ganglike characteristics reveals how Pentecostalism not only survives but actually thrives in Rio's prison subculture.

GANGS IN PRISON

The influence of narco-gangs like the Comando Vermelho in Rio's prisons cannot be overstated. In the same way that gangs control certain neighborhoods in the city, gangs control parts of Rio's jails and prisons. The primary difference is that the gang's power inside of prison is more concentrated and more totalitarian inside the cellblocks than it is outside. In Salgado Jail, more than half of the incarcerated residents are housed in a space that both the inmates and the guards refer to as the "Comando cells" because every inmate housed in those cells is under the direct control of the CV. Affiliation is reinforced every day at six o'clock, when the inmates in those cells pledge allegiance to the gang through their war cry, and during the rest of the day under direct control of gang leadership.

Gangs are the most powerful nonstate entity behind bars in Rio de Janeiro and they have created a social world that is largely beyond the reach of their captors. Prison guards and administrators dictate certain parts of prison life, but as an ex-inmate who spent nearly a decade living in the Comando Vermelho's cells inside a maximum security prison explained, "It isn't as if they [the state] don't have any power because they throw you in prison and do not let you leave, but once you are in the cellblocks, the guards do not interfere." Day-to-day life inside the cellblocks is only loosely monitored by prison authorities; the inmates themselves have a much stronger role in shaping order and routine.

Dr. Elizabeth Sussekind, a lawyer, university professor, and former Brazilian National Secretary of Justice, has been involved in the politics of Brazil's prison systems over the last four decades. She explained to me how gangs leverage the threat of violence to establish their control in the cellblocks:

> The penitentiaries are spaces controlled by gangs because everyone fears the gang leaders. The guards do not enter the cellblocks, because the state doesn't really equip them to go inside the cells, so they stay at the door. The guards have to enter unarmed, so they end up having to obey the gang leaders, because they walk around with concealed weapons and they have outside connections. They can use these connections to threaten the guards' families, and since the state doesn't protect its prison guards, the guards, well, not all of them, are silent about the violent threat of organized crime that exists inside of prison.

The war raging between the police and the gangs in Rio de Janeiro's *favelas* does not stop at the doors of the city's prisons and jails, and the guards at those facilities are fully aware that they could quickly become casualties in this conflict. Even though the gang members are imprisoned in state-run institutions, incarcerated gang members have access to a deadlier weapon cache than the unarmed guards. As a result, the guards know that they are outnumbered and outgunned if they walk through the cellblocks.

From the guards' perspective, the risks involved in establishing a presence inside the cellblocks do not outweigh the rewards, so they simply monitor from the perimeter. The guards do their best to reduce the number of escape attempts, but they are largely content to let the inmates sort things out for themselves inside the cells.

The scope of the gang's threat is not limited to violent action inside of the prison or jail buildings. Gang members inside of prison can access a sophisticated communication system that enables them to communicate between the prison and the street.

I found out how efficient the CV's communication system was when I spoke with Lucas, the former leader of Salgado's CV cells, while he was temporarily out of prison. We met in the food court of a shopping mall and traded stories over lunch about the jail and the status of shared acquaintances. After twenty minutes of catching up, he laughed to himself and started a new story by saying, "You never knew this, but—." Lucas proceeded to tell me about an escape attempt that was called off at the last minute in Salgado. He told me that his gang had procured a number of police uniforms[1] and planned to take advantage of the bare-bones weekend staff with a "Trojan horse–style" jailbreak.

Five CV members arrived at the jail dressed in civil police uniforms on a Saturday morning. They entered the building and started to talk with the two officers who were on duty as if they were part of the same police force. The CV members were able to enter the jail without a problem, but a group of volunteers from a church had arrived unexpectedly at the jail just minutes before. The volunteer group came every two weeks to conduct worship services with the inmates and provide them with basic medical care, but there was a miscommunication, and neither the prison staff nor the inmates knew the church group was coming on that Saturday. I was in Salgado that morning and remember the police officers talking to Salgado's staff members, but I didn't think anything of it at the time.

I don't know exactly how the CV members planned to get the inmates from the cells to the street—they could have forged a transfer order or they could have been planning to take hostages and demand that the cell door be opened under gunpoint. Whatever their plan was, it was cancelled when Lucas realized the volunteer group would be inside the prison during the escape.

Lucas told me that he frantically called a gang colleague outside of the facility from a cellphone and told him to call off the operation. The gang member who received Lucas's call then sent a message to the five CV members who were dressed as police officers and told them to abort the mission. In a testament to the effectiveness of the CV's communication system, the message was successfully sent from within Salgado's cellblocks to another gang member on the street and back to Salgado's entrance area within a few minutes. The five men in the stolen police uniforms left the prison as abruptly as they had arrived.

Lucas told me he called off the mission because they "didn't want to get you guys in the middle of anything." Though the escape failed, if at first you don't succeed, try and try again. The gang was persistent, and two weeks later the CV pulled off a successful jailbreak, and dozens of Comando Vermelho members, including Lucas, escaped. The second, successful attempt was possible with the help of a guard or staff member who likely received a hefty cash payoff.

Situations like these are not lost on the guards who work in Rio's jails and prisons. The police realize the walls of the institutions they monitor are porous, and gang leaders have access to information like guards' addresses, license plate numbers, and the routes they take to work, the gym, and their children's schools. So the guards must perform their jobs knowing that anything they do inside of prison can have dire consequences for themselves and their families once they punch out for the day. As a result of the constant threat looming over the individuals working in the prison system, the state has systematically relinquished some of its power to the gangs inside of prison.

PENTECOSTALS IN PRISON

Just like the gang, Pentecostal inmates control part of the prison. When Nestor, the Heroes of Christ's worship leader, surrendered to the police, he told me, "The first thing I did was to find the prison church. I knew that in basically every prison or jail, there is a church that is led by the prisoners." Over the last twenty years, these inmate-led churches have evolved from loosely organized groups of Pentecostal inmates into independent churches with congregations led by inmate pastors, deacons, secretaries, and worship teams. Even though these churches are not the products of prison ministries, and they do not have any formal denominational affiliation, there are prison churches like Heroes for Christ in every jail and prison in Rio de Janeiro.

Pentecostalism's presence in prison arose after gangs had firmly established their dominance in these places. This is important because Prison Pentecostalism began and grew in an environment controlled by narco-gangs. In the early 1990s, before the loosely organized groups of Pentecostals began to call themselves churches, they called themselves the "Comando de Cristo" or "Christ's Command," a direct riff on the most dominant prison gang, the Comando Vermelho, or Red Command. As the number of Pentecostals grew in the prison population, they began to organize themselves by borrowing organizational strategies from two sources: street churches like the Assemblies of God and prison gangs like the Comando Vermelho.

Pentecostal inmate groups followed the gang's lead and claimed part of the prison as their own. Just like there are "Comando cells," there are also the *celas dos irmãos*, or the "brothers' cells." The brothers' cells belong to the Pentecostals inside of prison. Thiago, a resident of these cells during his stint in the maximum-security prison Bangu, told me, "We lived together. The believers' cells were separate. Separate from those who did not have a commitment to God. It was the Pentecostals and the non-Pentecostals, you know?" In these cells, the Pentecostals called the shots, forming their own parallel power inside of prison.

The size and structure of the brothers' cells vary, depending on the institution. In some of the larger penitentiaries I visited, Pentecostal inmates controlled entire cellblocks, but inside the smaller, less stable jails, they owned a single cell or claimed part of a hallway as their own.

Cinza Penitentiary, one of the oldest and largest penitentiaries in Rio de Janeiro, was home to the best-organized and longest-running prison churches that I observed during my fieldwork. Close to 15 percent of Cinza's inmates lived in the brothers' cells at the end of the building's long corridor. They marked the beginning of their territory by painting the wall with an enormous mural that depicted Moses, staff in hand, crossing through a split Red Sea followed by dozens of Israelites. The bright, primary colors starkly contrasted with the faded gray, soot-stained walls of the building, and the words "Welcome to the Cinza Penitentiary Prison Church" were written in big block letters above the Old Testament scene. Adjacent to the church's cells was a chapel where the daily worship services and regular baptisms were held.

Not every prison church was able to create such a dramatic space as in Cinza. For example, because Salgado was packed to five or six times its intended capacity, there was not enough room for the prison church to have its own cell. Despite these constraints, owning space was still important to the prison church. Salgado's church, Heroes for Christ, claimed the final thirty feet at the end of the cellblock corridor as its own, and the inmates treated the space as sacred—an area separate from the rest of the profane jail. I asked the church's pastor about the space, and he told me,

> The church has to be respected, so I don't want anyone smoking in the church's space, because worship time is sacred. We see the respect they [inmates not affiliated with the church] have for us, a fear. The moment the service starts there is silence so they can hear the word, they put on their shirts and listen to God.

I was impressed and initially surprised that the other inmates in the cellblock complied with the Pentecostal inmates' expectations. What was in it for them? Inmates who had no intention of participating in the church's services still extinguished their cigarettes, put their shirts on, and, if there was room, retreated to their cells when the church brought out their Bibles and tambourines.

The members of the Cinza church also made their space sacred through a series of prohibitions and practices. Smoking, swearing, gambling, watching television, and drug use were not allowed in this space. The Pentecostal cells stood out from the other cells because the inmates kept the lights on during the day as opposed to the other cells that were purposefully kept dark to prevent anyone from observing what was happening inside the cells. Also, the pornography that served as the default wallpaper in the other cells was noticeably missing in the church-controlled wing.

PRISON PENTECOSTAL IDENTITY

Inside of prison, there was little doubt about which inmates belonged to the Pentecostal prison churches. In Cinza, inmates modified the obligatory white t-shirts by painting the church's logo—a Bible laid open with a dove flying through the bars of a prison cell window—on the front of their shirts to identify themselves as church members.

The t-shirts were a relatively new innovation; just a few years earlier, Pentecostal inmates wore suit jackets, slacks, and ties inside of prison garb. Marcio, an ex-inmate, told me that when he was incarcerated and living in the brothers' cells,

> A real Pentecostal was recognized by the way he dressed and the way he handled himself. You know the way that Pentecostals used to be? The ones that would not go swimming without wearing a shirt, or the ones that always wore slacks? Inside of prison, that is how a Pentecostal is recognized: long-sleeve shirt and slacks.

I asked for clarification: "The Pentecostal inmates wore these clothes inside of prison?" And he responded, "Exactly, we wore different clothes. We walked around activated." Inmates asked family members to bring in dress shirts, suit coats, ties, and slacks, and they wore them every day in prison, not just during the services, leaving no question about who was and was not a member of the prison church.

ORDER, NOT CHAOS

Even though the state had a very limited presence behind the locked prison doors, daily life in Rio's prisons was not chaotic. The gangs provided order and predictability by governing their space through enforcing their own laws and norms. Gang leaders dictated mundane details like who sleeps in the bunks versus the floor to weightier matters like issuing cellblock-wide orders to set fire to the mattresses during a riot. The Comando Vermelho instituted more than a set of do's and don'ts in their cells—they held their members to an ideology or moral code similar to the one they enforced in the neighborhoods they controlled. Their code demanded consistency in personal character, unwavering loyalty to the gang, absolute obedience to higher-ranking gang members, and a zero-tolerance policy for cooperating with the police.

The gang's moral code defined certain crimes as more respectable than others. Armed robberies, drug trafficking, and violence against the police were held in higher regard than grabbing the purse or cellphone of an unsuspecting victim. Though I never heard the Portuguese version of this phrase used, the notion of "honor among thieves" was an important component of the gang's ideology. Committing sexual crimes, particularly attacks against women and children, were considered the least honorable criminal acts and were not tolerated by the gangs in either the neighborhoods or cellblocks they controlled.

Gangs enforced their rules and maintained their power inside prison through a vertical hierarchal structure. The gang's leader was the most powerful inmate inside the prison; he was referred to as the "president." The president was appointed by the gang's institutional leadership and received information and commands from his superiors through text messages sent by smuggled cellphones, notes handed from family members during visiting hours, and inmates in transit. Or as Marcio said, "In prison there is a hierarchy, and you don't break that hierarchy."

Throughout the fieldwork, I spoke frequently with Lucas, the acting leader of the Comando Vermelho inside Salgado Jail and the man who told me about the failed escape plan that I unknowingly witnessed. He was in jail after being arrested for drug trafficking, possession of an illegal weapon, and involvement with organized crime. In Salgado, there was no doubt he was in charge of the Comando cells. Every time I entered the gang-controlled cells, he met me within a few feet of the cellblock's iron door and also made sure to escort me out of the cells when I left. Lucas wore the same white t-shirt and surf shorts as everyone else in the Comando cells, but his fellow inmates treated him much differently. Lucas could quiet the ever-present jailhouse cacophony by simply raising his voice. When he walked through the crowded hallway he never had to break stride because the other inmates stepped out of his way. Whenever I spoke with Lucas, his eyes rarely stopped scanning the other inmates in "his" cellblock, monitoring the movements of the nearly four hundred inmates in the five Comando Vermelho cells.

Lucas was always "on duty." If there were conflicts over food, bunk space, or a perceived insult, he had to directly intervene. He maintained contact with gang leaders on the street, and if his superiors sent a command, he had to make sure the task was successfully completed or he faced the consequences.

Lucas saw his role as gang leader as a way to bring order and relative peace to an inherently unpredictable, chaotic, and violent place. He told me,

> People out there think we are animals in here, raping and killing all day long. It's not like that, brother. There is respect in here. Everyone is on edge in here, but I don't let confrontations go beyond shouting. [Long pause] But there are times when I have to resolve some things.

I did not ask Lucas to clarify how he "resolved" the problems and conflicts in the CV cells, but the gang's set of rules that he enforced effectively eliminated much of the chaos that used to plague the prisons in the years before gang domination.

Though the Comando Vermelho's rules likely reduced random violence and uncertainty in the otherwise unmonitored cells, they did not make them entirely peaceful places. The punishments for breaking the rules were swift, violent, and often deadly. I heard from reliable sources about two inmates who were executed in the cellblocks in separate events by the Comando Vermelho for violating the gang's rules. One was strangled and the other injected with a lethal dose of narcotics to make the death look like an overdose. I did not ask the gang-affiliated inmates I spoke with about these killings, so I don't know for certain that they happened or who was involved, but the fear of being judged and executed by the gang was a consistent theme in the interviews I conducted with ex-inmates.

Junho, for example, had no doubt that his life rested in the hands of his gang's leaders during two prison sentences that swallowed up his late teens and most of his twenties. He served his first sentence after being arrested with cocaine and a handgun outside of a Samba club in Niterói, across the Guanabara Bay from downtown Rio de Janeiro. "I got caught with forty packages of cocaine, a machine gun called an Uru, two transmitter radios, and corruption of a minor [he had a younger boy working for him]. I got ten years, six months, it made me think it was the end of the world, you know? I was stuck inside prison, just a crazy eighteen-year-old guy, a crazy guy stuck in jail."

Junho served his first sentence, but after his release he didn't stay out of trouble for long. As he told me, "I got out, took a breath and went right back in again." Eight months after he was released, Junho was arrested while he was leaving a late-night card game. He was carrying a gun that he won in the game and was shot in the leg by the police during the arrest.

When I spoke with him, Junho had finished his second prison term and had been living on the outside for over a year, but he told me that he still had nightmares about his close call with a Comando Vermelho "jury" during his second prison stay. The jury is one mechanism the gang uses to enforce obedience to their rules inside of prison, Junho explained:

> Inside of prison, the Comando Vermelho has a leader who decides what happens to the people in there. Just like the church has a pastor who leads his church, the gang has a guy, their president, who was responsible for the 1,400 men in prison, who is responsible for everyone. The president has his group and they "solve problems" within the prison, you know? They take the guy who they think has done something and put him in a kind of a trial. They grab you, see what you have done, judge you, and sentence you.

Shortly after Junho began his second stint in prison, a young man arrived from his neighborhood and accused him of giving the police information that led to his arrest. Junho rubbed his chin and shook his head as he told me the story: "I was stuck, like a caged bird. This guy is accusing me of ratting on him and there is no forgiving a rat in the Comando Vermelho."

Junho's fellow gang member publicly accused him of talking to the police, one of the most heinous offenses in the gang's eyes. Since both Junho and his accuser were housed in the Comando cells, the issue was brought to the gang leaders for resolution. The gang's leader presided as judge and communicated with Comando Vermelho members on the street who were familiar with the events surrounding Junho's arrest. Fortunately for Junho, the witnesses corroborated his version of the story, and his life was spared. But his case is an example of how the gang governs its space and enforces the top-down parallel power structure they have constructed in prison. The relationship between the gang leaders and the inmates living in their cells was a simple one for Junho: "You have to do whatever he [the gang leader] says, get it? If you don't, you will end up dying in that place."

When Junho described the gang leader's role in prison, he compared it to a pastor. "Just like the church has a pastor who leads his church," he said, "the gang has a guy who was responsible for the 1,400 men in prison." The comparison makes sense from an inmate's perspective because both the prison pastor and prison gang leader are visible, influential leaders inside of prison. In the prisons I studied, the pastor was the "boss" of the Pentecostal cells: He did the bulk of the preaching, organized communion, led the worship services, prayed before important rituals, and managed the church's leadership team. His duties extended beyond leading the religious rituals in prison, because he was also in charge of enforcing the church's rules and regulations.

The prison churches elect their leaders democratically. Incarcerated members of the church choose who will serve as the pastor, deacon, secretary, and worship leader. Cristiano said, "We vote based on how the brother lives day to day, his contribution to the work, the example he has given; this is what matters." These elections are very different than national political campaigns: the candidates are judged on their day-to-day lives, not their words.

In the most organized churches an elected assistant supported every leadership position. In the Cinza church, for example, there was a secretary and an assistant secretary working for the church. They were in charge of the church's finances and keeping track of the members and visitors. When I first attended a service at Cinza, I signed a guestbook that had cataloged the names and home churches of over a decade's worth of visitors. During the service, the secretary handed me a personalized welcome letter signed by both him and the pastor. If the active secretary were released or transferred, the assistant secretary (who had by this time been trained for the position) would be promoted to be acting secretary and an election would be held among the inmates to elect the next assistant secretary.

Belonging to either a prison gang or a prison church requires submission to authority. Junho survived his moment in front of the Comando Vermelho's jury, but after his public conversion at a Pentecostal outreach service in prison, he moved his personal belongings to the Pentecostal cells and immediately became subject to a new authority, the prison church leadership. Junho said that the inmates in the brothers' cells welcomed him, but the transition proved difficult because of the disciplined lifestyle, rigorous prayer routines, daily worship services, and required Bible studies.

On top of the rigorous schedule, the marijuana he used to smoke throughout the day to take the edge off prison life was no longer an option for him. Junho butted heads with his new cellmates and church leaders during the first few weeks after his conversion. When the conflict became more serious, one of the church deacons confronted Junho, pulled him aside, and told him in no uncertain terms, "The key to being a believer inside prison is a simple one: obedience. You can't be a believer without obeying. If you are not obeying the leadership of your pastor, you are disobeying God." Junho's new set of leaders operated by a different set of rules and a different set of values than the gang, but they expected everyone in their space to submit to their authority with the same unquestioning devotion and loyalty.

FORGIVABLE SINS?

In prison subculture, sexual assault rivaled "ratting" to the police as the worst act someone could commit. Men convicted of pedophilia or rape were subject to two separate punishments—one ordered by the judge and another ordered by his fellow inmates when he arrived in prison. Inside the penal institutions in my study, the second judgment, enforced by the inmates, ranged from total social exclusion and isolation, to torture and execution.

I met inmates whose teeth had been shattered in beatings they received on their first night in prison because of the crime they had committed against a woman on the street. Others had been severely burned by their fellow inmates as a post-sentencing punishment. Inmates accused of sexual offenses are sometimes killed the day they arrive in jail and never make it to trial. There can be considerable social pressure on an inmate to avenge an attack on someone from his neighborhood, especially if the attacker is placed in the same cellblock.

In prisons throughout Brazil sexual offenders are treated as less than human by other inmates and sometimes used as pawns in never-ending battles between the inmates and the prison administration. During a prison riot in São Luis, a city in northern Brazil, inmates took control of the facility and held guards and maintenance staff hostage. To catch the media's attention and show the administration that their demands were serious, the rioting inmates decapitated seven fellow prisoners, who had all been convicted of child rape.[2]

The inmates' complaints and demands centered on the conditions of the facility, overcrowding, poor food, and visiting schedule. In fact, the riot had nothing to do with child abuse or child abusers, but inside a Brazilian prison the life of an individual convicted of sexually abusing a child is essentially worthless. Even if such offenders survived the first few days in prison and absorbed the beatings and other punishments, their lives were always at risk.

The prison churches did not participate in the jailhouse beatings of convicted and accused sex offenders. If an inmate was able to survive long enough to join the Pentecostal church, he could avoid the vigilante justice dished out in the cellblocks. Knowing what I do about prison subculture in Rio de Janeiro, if I were accused of a sexual offense and thrown into prison, the first thing I would do once I heard the iron door slam behind me would be to seek out the prison church, because in general the men living in the brothers' cells were left out of prison violence and were protected by their affiliation with the Pentecostals. This sort of protection would be especially useful for convicted sex offenders, given their vulnerable status in the prison population.

I asked the acting pastor of Heroes for Christ whether he could explain why his church offered protection to these inmates who have been convicted of these highly stigmatized crimes. More specifically, I asked him to respond to the critique that his church was used as a refuge for inmates convicted of sexual crimes. He acknowledged that church membership would be an appealing alternative for this type of inmate and offered a theological defense of his organization's willingness to accept the sexual offender:

> The reality of prison life is that being caught with a 214, penal code 214, which is rape or pedophilia, is not accepted inside of prison. The person arrested for this crime is not well received here. So the church works with the word of God, because to God a little lie is the same as a big lie, sins don't have different sizes. Getting caught with a 155 [theft], may not have a long prison sentence, but to God there is no difference between that and abusing a life, being a pedophile.... I keep hitting this point with them that God loves the prostitute, God loves the rapist, God doesn't love their attitude, the sin he commits, but God is there with open arms to transform them into a new creation.

Most members of the prison churches are not serving time for sex-related crimes, but no matter the type of conviction, joining a Pentecostal inmate community isn't simply a free pass for a threatened inmate; it requires a twenty-four-hour-a-day, seven-day-a-week commitment, and there are consequences for disobedience. The prison church pastor told me, "If a member is not obeying the rules and norms of the church, if he is not adapting, he will be taken out as quickly as he was let in. You can't hurt the church's work." Joining a prison church was not a free pass through prison life, because it carried its own set of rules and punishments.

At Cinza, a Pentecostal pastor who regularly visited the inmates told me that earlier in the year a man living in the Pentecostal cells was caught sexually abusing a younger, weaker church member. The abuse went undetected for a few weeks, but when church leaders discovered it, they immediately removed the offender from their community. The church's punishment did not stop at simple expulsion: The pastor went to the prison administration to explain what the man had done and demanded that the man be transferred. The administration took the request seriously, and the offending Pentecostal member was quickly moved to another prison. It was not a random transfer. The inmate judged guilty by the church was sent to the most dangerous wing of Rio's most notorious prison. From the way the story was explained to me, such a transfer was essentially a death sentence. The protection offered by church affiliation can be pulled away if an individual strays from the expectations. If the offense is serious, like cooperating with the police or sexually abusing a weaker person, the consequences will likely be serious as well, even deadly.

TWO VERSIONS OF MASCULINITY

Conceptions of masculinity were an important part of prison subculture in both the gang-controlled cells and the Pentecostal cells. Men's jails and prisons are unique places to study gender because the institutions consist exclusively of men, and there are competing conceptualizations of masculinity behind bars.

There are important differences between these conceptualizations, but each insists that the mothers, wives, and girlfriends of fellow inmates must be treated with respect. I learned about this important part of inmate subculture while living inside the cellblocks at the APAC prison in Minas Gerais. That particular prison had a conjugal visit program that allowed an inmate to spend private time once a month with his wife or girlfriend in a separate room in the facility. One afternoon while I was talking with five men in the prison hallway, an inmate's wife arrived for her scheduled visit. Since I was not on the conjugal visit schedule myself, I was unaware of the protocol surrounding these visits until one of the inmates literally pulled me by my shirtsleeve so I would not be in the hallway when the woman arrived. The six of us huddled together in the corner and remained out of sight until she passed through the hallway and entered the private room. We hid so the visitor would not have to worry about being ogled by inmates or suffer any sort of additional shame or embarrassment by visiting her loved one in prison.

I was grateful that I learned this lesson early in the project, so I knew how to appropriately interact during family visits or while waiting in the visiting line alongside the inmates' wives and girlfriends. I made a habit of never speaking to an inmate's wife, mother, or girlfriend unless she was personally introduced to me.

The gang promoted a particular archetype of masculinity in prison that was an extra-strength version of *machismo*. The gang members treated mothers, wives, and sisters of other inmates with respect, but they objectified women in general through the sexually explicit music they played and composed in the cells, the hundreds of pornographic images pasted on the walls, and their own informal, after-hours visitor schedule. During the evenings, pornographic videos played on the television sets in the CV-controlled cells, and I heard stories at a number of facilities about how inmates hired erotic dancers to perform in the hallway just outside of the cells.

In fact, women frequently visited the prisons and jails outside of official visiting hours. During the evenings, when few guards were on duty (sometimes only one), inmates with enough clout and enough cash to pay a bribe to the guard called in their wives, girlfriends, and prostitutes to visit jail. Unlike the APAC system, in Salgado a fee paid directly to the guards bought the paying inmate admission for a woman visitor and half an hour or so of private, uninterrupted use of a closet in the administration office—the same space where I conducted the interviews during the day. In the CV cellblocks it was no secret who was able to spend time in the rented closet space, and even though they were incarcerated, men bragged about how many women they were able to bring into the facility.

I did not ask any inmates about homosexual practice inside of the cellblocks. In Salgado, Lucas, the Comando Vermelho leader, told me that the gang did not accept homosexuality, and I knew of only one openly gay inmate living in the gang-controlled cells. When he arrived, he was not beaten or sent out of the cells, because his crime was not of a sexual nature, but he was treated like a leper. This inmate was given a cup that he could use for water and his own bar of soap then was subsequently treated as if he was contaminated with an infectious disease. The inmates actively ignored him, and nobody in the gang's cells was allowed to touch him or even talk to him. I do not know if this sort of treatment was unique to Salgado—I heard that there are different arrangements in the penitentiaries—but it fit the hypermasculine identity that pervaded the prison subculture.

The masculinity promoted in the Pentecostal cells was very different from the version that prevailed in the gang's cells. Most obviously, porn, strippers, and sexually explicit funk music were strictly off-limits in the Pentecostal cells. But more meaningfully, the Pentecostal inmates used a different criterion to judge what it means to be a successful man. In *Reforming Machismo: Evangelical Conversion and Gender in Colombia*, the author Elizabeth Brusco argues that Pentecostal practice directs men's time, energy, resources, and emotions into the domestic sphere as opposed to the street. She emphasized that the Pentecostal interpretation of manhood runs counter to the dominant cultural machismo:

> The machismo role and the male role defined by evangelicalism are almost diametrical opposites. Aggression, violence, pride, self-indulgence, and an individualistic orientation in the public sphere are replaced by peace seeking, humility, self-restraint, and a collective orientation and identity within the church and the home. (137)

Brusco argues that the machismo version of masculinity is "over the long run, very demanding and difficult for all under its sway, including the males who must perform this role" (120). The Pentecostal ideal of masculinity may or may not be a relief to the pressure put on men by the machismo model, but it is at least a viable option. Brusco argues that Pentecostalism reshapes gender roles in converts' homes not by empowering women to challenge their place in society, but by changing men's understandings of their roles at home and in the world.

Inside of prison, Pentecostal inmates used their countercultural frame of masculinity as an important identity marker. Men would often weep openly and unashamedly during the worship services. Unlike the tough, emotionally detached presentations I observed in the gang cells, the Pentecostal inmates frequently hugged each other during and after prayer. During the testimonies they shared in the worship services, inmates routinely admitted feeling fear about the future and remorse about how they had prioritized other pursuits in front of their family.

I observed one of the most compelling examples of using masculinity as a marker of Pentecostal affiliation when Lucas, the CV leader in Salgado, went through a gradual conversion, or return to, Christianity. Because of his position in the gang, I wasn't able to record a private interview with him—the guards would not allow it—but I spoke with him every time I entered the CV cells, and our conversations grew longer and more in-depth as he began to trust me. If Lucas made a public, dramatic conversion, I missed it, but his increased participation with the Pentecostal visitors in the gang-controlled cells he controlled was unmistakable. I first noticed Lucas's change in behavior when he started to stand on the outside edge of the circle during the worship services held in the CV cells. Over the next days and weeks he began to migrate toward the center of the circle and participate openly by singing, clapping, raising his arms during the songs, and listening intently during the sermons and testimonies.

During this time, the content of my private conversations with Lucas changed—most notably he told me that he was now "walking with God." I spoke with other CV inmates who told me that Lucas had stopped the drug traffic inside of the jail and no longer took his share of the profits from that enterprise. Lucas didn't publicly disavow his role as gang leader or ask to be moved to the Pentecostal cell in the other wing of Salgado, as was the usual practice. Because of his position in the gang, he had to navigate variables that other less-visible inmates did not have to confront. I also believe that Lucas knew an escape plan was brewing, and his time at Salgado was coming to an end. He planned to make his exit from the gang once he was on the outside.

Lucas made a public profession of faith during an afternoon worship service led by a husband-wife-daughter trio from a Deus é Amor (God Is Love) church, located less than a mile from the jail. After the singing had ended and the testimonies began, Lucas stepped toward the middle of the two dozen inmates and asked if he could share something with the group. Lucas had an arm draped around the shoulders of an inmate on his right during other testimonies and before he started to speak, he wrapped his other arm around an inmate on his left.

He addressed the group with both of his arms draped over the shoulders of his fellow inmates, and every eye in the room was fixed on him. The CV prisoners were completely silent and hung on his every word. In the dozens of services I attended in Salgado, no group had listened to anyone as intently as the other CV inmates listened to Lucas. He started by saying, "I arrived in prison, just like many of you—we are the same. I arrived full of hate. I am a human being, and you know I am not perfect. Only God and his son Jesus are perfect, but God is working in me, and I have changed."

The evidence he used to support this change was that he used to have two lovers, but now he "only looked at his wife." The inmates likely knew about his affairs because of the after-hours visiting system in Salgado. Lucas continued by telling the group, "If you receive a visit today from your mom or wife, make sure that the first thing you do is say 'I love you.'" He added, "You know how much suffering we have caused and how much time they have spent on their knees praying for us."

He spoke for at least ten minutes and told the men that it was time for them to change their lives. He told them specifically not to go back to the drug trade when they left Salgado and implored the men in the group to seek God's forgiveness. "You could have killed one hundred people, but Jesus will forgive you. He is there knocking at the door. He knocked at the door of my life and I let him in; I have changed and you can, too. Let him in."

Lucas's public confession included a call for his fellow gang members to follow his lead in two specific ways. The first was not to go back to the drug dens, which meant leaving the gang. The second was to change the way they treated the women in their lives. He used his own recommitment to his wife and his abandonment of his extramarital relationships as an example of what it means to be a man.

A GANG-FLAVORED FAITH

The hands-off approach implemented by the guards in Rio's prisons and jails provided an interesting context to study religion because the environment was unregulated by outside forces and the jailhouse churches were not directed by an outside prison ministry. The role of visiting Pentecostal volunteers was an important part of Prison Pentecostalism, but these groups did not implement or direct a formal prison ministry or any sort of ongoing programming inside prison. The inmates were the ones who created the organizational structure of the Pentecostal groups active in the prisons and they borrowed heavily from the gangs' organizational model.

The Prison Pentecostalism I studied in Rio de Janeiro would have looked very different if directed by formal prison ministries or a state-sponsored chaplain. Given the stigma of gangs in larger society, the prison ministries or chaplain would have likely been uncomfortable starting or supporting Pentecostal groups that shared so many characteristics with the gangs. Repurposing gang rituals like the aggressive "war cry" depicted at the beginning of this chapter is just one example of a ritual that would likely have been frowned on by an outside program intent on persuading men to abandon their gang affiliation and cultural habits.

Prison ministries and state-affiliated chaplains rely on teachers and leaders who are not incarcerated. It is impossible to guess which inmates would rise to leadership positions if an outside group had been involved inside the jails and prisons I studied, but they would likely be different than the leaders voted into power directly by the inmates. The Pentecostal inmates valued the way a person lived his day-to-day life behind bars, and since they were incarcerated together, their position provided an unrivaled perspective from which to observe an inmate's character and devotion. A prison ministry operated from outside prison could not make these sorts of evaluations.

Finally, outside Pentecostal churches would not have had the same standing among the inmates as the groups the inmates created and maintained because they would not have arisen from within the cellblocks. The prison church structure and the function that prison churches served made sense in the prison environment in a way that would have been impossible to re-create on the outside. It is very difficult to convey the depth of authenticity these groups had created inside the cellblocks.

This context also provides a unique addition to the previous literature on Pentecostalism's success on the marginalized fringes of Latin American society. None of the inmates I spoke with had taken college-level courses, and the vast majority of the prison church members had been involved in illegal activity not long before they joined the church or were elected into leadership positions. Surely some of the men in the prison had been wrongly incarcerated, but I met very few men who claimed to be completely innocent of wrongdoing.

Yet despite their lack of formal education and their involvement in crime, very effective leaders emerged from this group. Rio's prison churches give a clear example of how the faith can empower indigenous leadership, even when the individuals in a given group are among society's most stigmatized people. Moreover, Pentecostalism favors the sort of charismatic authority that is difficult, if not impossible, to teach in the classroom. The leadership qualities held by many of the prison church leaders are also useful in a narco-gang, so it should not be surprising that gang leaders like Lucas could transition to new roles as religious leaders almost seamlessly.

Prison churches like Heroes for Christ and the Cinza church affirmed the dignity of the men who participated in them, even though the groups shared some structural and functional characteristics with the gangs that operated alongside of them. Though the bodies of the church members were incarcerated, and their life choices were severely limited by their imprisonment, they could for the most part choose to join or not to join the group.

The leaders to whom they submitted were elected from within the group, not assigned by the prison administration or any outside group, so the members and leaders alike had ownership of these churches. As Cristiano, the pastor of Heroes for Christ, said, "The church is ours. It belongs to those of us on the inside." Just as important, the prison church members held one another to a strict moral code. Though their status as inmates carried tremendous social stigma outside prison, behind bars this code provided an opportunity for inmates to act morally and participate in an activity that they perceived as honorable. Finally, the Pentecostal churches preached a message of redemption and that held that even those who had been convicted of despicable acts were not lost causes, but worthy of redemption.

CHAPTER 5

PRISON PENTECOSTALISM

A FAITH PRACTICED

"Have you confessed your sins?" Six men draped in white baptismal robes replied to the pastor's question with affirmative nods. The pastor continued, "Baptism is a symbolic bath. You will enter the water as that man you used to be and when you rise, you will rise as a new man. Today, something beautiful is happening in your lives."

When the pastor finished, the first inmate stepped toward the bulging, blue plastic wading pool assembled on the floor of Salgado Jail. The prisoner sat down in the knee-high water, bowed his head, and clenched his hands together in a position of prayer. The pastor placed two hands on the sitting man's head and began to pray. With the prayer's final phrase, "In the name of the Father, the Son, and the Holy Spirit," the pastor lowered the inmate's head and shoulders toward the water and submerged the incarcerated body into the improvised baptismal pool. Underwater for just a moment, the inmate emerged baptized to the sound of fifty of his fellow inmates clapping their hands and yelling out "Amen!" "Alleluia!" and "Gloria a Deus!"

The newly baptized young man made a very public profession of faith by being baptized at the ceremony inside the jail. The ritual symbolized his belief in a set of basic Christian theological tenets concerning the nature of God, sin, repentance, Jesus, forgiveness, and the afterlife. The baptism presented an opportunity to embody his new identity as a Pentecostal inside of prison. I like to think of the prison churches as the fireplace, the inmate members as the wood or the fuel, and the practices and rituals, conversion, baptism, worship, praise, acts of self-sacrificial generosity, and love toward others as the visible flames.

CONVERSION

Most inmates convert or recommit their lives to God inside of prison. I didn't speak with any prison church member who said they were content with their religious lives during the time of their arrests. Junho is an example of a prisoner who converted to Pentecostalism inside of prison. He grew up on one of Rio's roughest edges and was familiar with the basics of the Pentecostal faith, but as a teenager his interests gravitated toward another local institution, the Comando Vermelho. He started selling cocaine in his teens and like many young men in the *favelas* who participate in the drug trade, he was arrested and sent to prison before he turned twenty.

While he was in prison Junho stayed loyal to the gang and deepened his involvement in the organization. He was released but didn't last long on the streets. He was the one who told me, "I got out of prison, took a breath, and went right back in." Actually, Junho took eight months of breaths outside of prison before he was once again arrested. Just like his first arrest, he was again busted for drug trafficking and weapons charges, but his second stint in prison started in the hospital as his femur, shattered by bullets fired by the arresting police officers, healed.

Locked up again, Junho's indifference toward Pentecostalism dissipated when his life was threatened, this time by his own gang. Shortly after he left the hospital and landed in his cell, he was accused by a fellow CV member of cooperating with the police, a capital offense in the gang's eyes. I described his "trial" in front of the Comando Vermelho leadership in the last chapter, and though Junho was cleared of any wrongdoing, his close call with jailhouse justice inspired him to reevaluate his life, especially his affiliation with the CV. "I realized that to the Comando Vermelho, you're like a disposable cup in their hands. Actually to any gang, it really doesn't matter which one. When you are no longer useful to them, the first time you waver, if you hesitate, you are as good as dead."

Sweating out the hours around his trial, wondering if he would make it through the day, convinced Junho that there were some serious drawbacks to gang life. "I started to realize that things weren't working for me anymore. I sat on my bed and I thought, wait a minute, I am back in prison, I have been shot, my leg is full of iron, what am I doing, man?" On top of the looming threat of being executed at the hands of members of his gang and a left leg that would never fully heal, Junho realized that he wasn't getting rich as a CV member as he had hoped he would. While on the streets, he had access to plenty of cash, certainly more than if he worked the same number of hours at a formal job, but he had been in prison for most of his twenties. While he was sitting in his cell physically and financially broken, he pondered his life and concluded that his CV affiliation had cost him much more than it had given him. So Junho made a decision, "I'm going to join the church, man. I'm going to start following the Bible. Why should I keep living like this?"

Junho made his decision to convert to Pentecostalism while he was sitting in his jail cell by himself, but he acted on his private decision by participating in a public ritual in the adjacent cellblock during which he made a commitment to God in front of his peers. Junho responded to the prison pastor's call, raised his hand, prayed with the members of the prison church, and gave his life to God. He followed that public decision by packing up his belongings in his CV cell and moving into the brothers' cells.

I asked Junho what his friends and colleagues in the gang thought of his decision. He told me they were less than encouraging:

Huh! They [his former gang colleagues] ripped the heck out of me, they ripped the heck out of me. It was crazy difficult. No one wants to talk to you any more, they think that you've changed, "Ah, you know that thing happened with him and now he's hiding behind the Bible." They told me, "Let's see if you keep this up on the outside; here on the inside being a believer's easy," and so on.

Junho's conversion was especially easy to ridicule because it immediately followed his trial with the gang, and the Pentecostals offered the best way to escape a deadly situation. But as a group, inmates let a person's actions speak and they watched to see how Junho lived after his conversion. One of the easiest things for the gang to monitor was Junho's postconversion drug use. Once a daily marijuana user and dedicated cocaine aficionado, Junho stopped using drugs cold turkey. The CV controlled the intra-prison drug market, so even if Junho wanted to use discreetly, the gang would have known about it, and if he had continued to use there would have been dire consequences.

Quitting dope was just part of Junho's Pentecostal practice; changing his wardrobe was another. "I got a suit and a tie inside and I started to preach inside of prison." Junho's suit and tie announced his new identity to everyone, including himself. Preaching to his fellow inmates was yet another. "We would go out all day preaching in the middle of the cellblock. We evangelized all 1,400 men [living in the prison] ... and we won a lot of souls. We took a lot of souls out of Satan's hands. Every day it was me and two other guys, and God knows where they walk now, hopefully they are well." Junho was transformed from an active gang member to a preaching Pentecostal in just a few weeks.

His public practice was the visible side of his new faith, but he told me that when he was alone in his cell, he deepened his understanding of Pentecostal Christianity by reading the Bible. "I made a commitment to God that I would study the Bible. So I studied, studied, studied, studied, and studied!" Junho had excellent verbal communication skills. During the interview I would ask him one simple question and he would respond with five- and ten-minute answers. The two interviews I recorded with Junho filled more than a dozen single-spaced pages when transcribed. But Junho's reading and studying skills were not as developed. He had dropped out of school well before graduation and told me he had never studied a subject like he studied the Bible in prison. His studying deepened his understanding of his religion, but it also affirmed his new identity as a Pentecostal and not a gang member.

"Man, I'd never seen myself like that before," he said. "I started to see that I was different, and when my mother came to visit, even she saw that I was different."

Junho reported that practicing his faith not only changed the way others viewed him but his self-perception also changed over time. His conversion during the worship service was certainly an important moment in his life, but wearing different clothes, studying the Bible, and quitting drugs were in his mind evidence of a real conversion. The Pentecostal practices gave him a platform to *be* a new person, not just say he was transformed.

Other inmates, like Pedro, converted to Pentecostalism before he landed in jail, in his case Salgado. He had been a leader in a small Assemblies of God church located in a poor neighborhood on the western outskirts of Rio de Janeiro. The pastor had taken him under his wing, mentored him, and was preparing him to take over the church once he retired. In spite of Pedro's limited education, his pastor recognized his potential as a communicator and told him he had a God-given gift to preach, so he worked with Pedro on his sermons and delivery. Pedro developed his craft on the street corners and public spaces of Rio de Janeiro as well as from the pulpit of the church. But his religious career abruptly changed direction when he decided to participate in a "one-time, no one gets hurt" burglary with a team of thieves to supplement his meager salary as a construction worker.

The first job was successful—they stole what they wanted and nobody was physically hurt. But Pedro strayed from the "one-time" part of his original plan when the group called about the next job. Pedro accepted the offer, and the "one-time" criminal activity turned into two, then three, then more times.

When Pedro began working with the burglary crew, he didn't want anyone else to know, so he drifted from the church and started to live a double life in order to keep his criminal activity hidden. He held it together for over a year, but his world came crashing down when he was arrested after the botched robbery of a jewelry store and thrown into a cell at Salgado. He told me, "When I landed inside here, I thought it was over. I lost my family, I lost my dignity, my identity. I thought about taking my own life."

When I interviewed Pedro, he had been in prison for eight months. During our conversation he started to choke on his words and tears welled up in his eyes when he told me how hard it was to face his former pastor, his mentor, who still visited him regularly at Salgado. Pedro's watery eyes transitioned into shoulder-shaking sobs when he told me his wife was pursuing a divorce and that he was losing his family.

Pedro's commitment—or, in his case, recommitment—to faith came during a serious life crisis. I asked him to explain how he returned to his faith:

> On April 27, I decided to go to the worship service here in the jail. I used to be a street preacher, but I had gone away from God's plan for my life. In the worship service in prison the Word of God touched me deeply. At the end of the sermon, the pastor asked, "Do you want to reconcile with God? Now is your chance." God spoke to my heart in that moment and I confessed to God what I had done and how I had disobeyed his word and sinned against my family and against my wife. I cried like a child. I went to the worship service the next day with the desire to undo the things I had done.

Pedro's jailhouse religious recommitment rejuvenated a faith practice that had grown stale during the months leading up to his arrest. His emotional plea to God was an attempt to restore the dignity he had lost. His tearful commitment to God in Salgado marked a return to, as opposed to an initial conversion to, the faith.

As a recommitted Pentecostal, he wasn't starting from the beginning. When I first saw Pedro preach in the cellblock, it was clear that he had done this before. He was a skilled preacher and knew how to transition through the different stages of a worship service. Just weeks after his arrest, he was elected as the head pastor for the Heroes for Christ Prison Church.

Though Pedro had experience and skills that would help the church, he had to do more than break down and cry to convince his cellmates that his recommitment was sincere. Pedro's tears were not the first ones that his cellmates had seen. Tears of remorse were not scarce commodities in the jail cells, so the inmates watched how Pedro lived his life in the jail and eventually voted for him based on his postcommitment actions.

I recorded dozens of Pentecostal conversion narratives throughout the fieldwork. Taken together, the interviews make for a dramatic collection. The conversion stories were filled with guns, drugs, sex, heartbreak, gangs, poverty, and a vibrant spiritual yearning. Mateus's testimony stood out because it had a bit of everything, plus he has the distinction of converting while a prisoner, but not in prison.

Mateus was born in Cidade de Deus (City of God)—a neighborhood made famous by the critically acclaimed 2003 film of the same name—and joined the Comando Vermelho as a teenager. He became a local celebrity in his early twenties after he committed a series of brazen carjackings that were immortalized in a funk song by a local songwriter. The song painted Mateus as a fearless carjacker with a knack for escaping from the police in the fancy imported cars he stole. He became a sort of CV folk hero, and as the song became more popular at CV parties, people began to call him "Bad Bullet," borrowing a phrase from the song.

Mateus didn't get to enjoy the fruits of his celebrity status for very long. He was arrested and imprisoned after a shootout with the police that left his friend dead and Mateus looking at ten years in a maximum-security penitentiary. Inside prison, Mateus's gang career continued to flourish, and after a few years he was promoted to leader of the Comando Vermelho cellblock. He told me, "My gang career really started in there; that is where it all happened. I had power in prison; I was the one who resolved the problems."

After serving seven years of his sentence, he was granted a day of home leave. He would have one every month, per Brazilian penal law, but in Mateus's mind, his first day of home leave would mark his last day in prison, because he had no intention of returning. He had been promoted by the Comando Vermelho and was given control of a drug-distribution point and the surrounding neighborhood. "I would be like a general manager," he told me. "The community would be under my responsibility—no murder, no theft, no attitude

could be taken without me giving my permission. I had this responsibility inside the prison, and I was going to have the same responsibility on the outside." Mateus was ready to be the boss and had no
plans to leave gang life, so serving the last few years of his sentence
seemed like a joke.

But Mateus's home-leave plans changed abruptly after he received
some unsettling news: his girlfriend had started dating another man.
On the day he was released, the pain of the perceived betrayal burned in
Mateus hotter than his desire to start his new job as a local crime boss.
Mateus's girlfriend had a religious experience while he was locked up
and had recently checked into a residential Pentecostal rehabilitation
facility in order to confront a drug addiction. He had been obsess-
ing over the situation for weeks and instead of going straight to the
Complexo de Alemão to meet the CV leaders, he headed toward the
recovery center. Mateus explained his state of mind that day: "I was
taken by a force, by grief, by rage, and I went to the church instead.
I was going to kill her."

He arrived at the recovery center armed and angry. He stood at
the gate yelling his girlfriend's name until the church's pastor met
him with some yelling of his own. The confrontation escalated when
Mateus used his CV status to try to intimidate the pastor, but the pastor did not wilt under the threats, nor did he call the police. In fact,
he matched Mateus's increasing aggression by shoving his finger into
Mateus's chest and telling him that he knew who he was and why he
was there and that Mateus had no right for "revenge," given his own
unfaithfulness in the relationship.

Mateus said that something happened while they were shouting at
each other. The rage within him subsided, in a way he couldn't fully
explain. He decided to relinquish his weapon and then he accepted the
pastor's offer to leave the entrance gate and come into his office. Inside
the pastor's office, the two men spoke, and Mateus decided to submit
his life to God. When I asked him how he made the decision, he said,
"The pastor put his hands on my head, prayed, and cast out the entire
legion of demons that were attached to my life. I was released and
I began to see clearly that God could change my life."

By anyone's measure, Mateus had had quite a day. He woke up, left prison for the first time in seven years with the intention of flouting the terms of his release and taking on a new post with the CV. Then he tried to kill his girlfriend, changed his mind, and converted to Pentecostal Christianity, all within a few hours. On top of that, he reported that a Pentecostal pastor had freed him from a legion of demons. But his day wasn't finished. Mateus faced a serious decision: Would he go back to prison? That morning he woke up thinking he was done with prison, but after a very eventful day that culminated in his conversion, he faced a choice that seriously tested his newfound faith. Mateus told me, "I opened my heart and received the Word, so I returned to jail together with the team from the church. They brought me back to jail." Conversion is often the easiest part of being a Pentecostal, and for Mateus, living out his conversion meant going back to prison.

When I met Mateus, he had finished his prison sentence, reconciled with his girlfriend, married her, and was working full time at the recovery center where he made his dramatic conversion. There is a tendency in Pentecostal conversion narratives to emphasize and sometimes sensationalize the "sinfulness" of the convert's past in order to highlight the postconversion change. Aware of this tendency, I pushed Mateus on the details, because even for Pentecostal prison conversions, his story was dramatic.

Mateus knew what was driving my questions, so he took out his phone and showed me a series of photos and videos taken on the day in question. The people at the recovery center also thought that it was a day to remember because they took dozens of photos and videos with their cellphones and later shared them with him. Mateus showed me a series of photos of a much skinnier version of himself standing next to the pastor outside of his office and another of him surrounded by praying church members. He flipped through more scenes from the church until he got to another photo taken inside the van on the way back to prison, then pulled up a video clip of him leaving the van accompanied by a half a dozen church members. The video showed Mateus hugging each one of them just outside the prison door before he returned to his cell.

The prison context can serve as a greenhouse for inmates' Pentecostal lives. Their faith can grow very fast inside of prison because many Pentecostal inmates are thrust into leadership positions that would likely not be available to them if they were members of churches outside of prison.

LOVE YOUR BROTHER

One of Prison Pentecostalism's requirements is to abstain from "sinful" behavior, which prompted Junho, for example, to quit using drugs. Another aspect of the lifestyle that is just as essential to the practice of the faith is unity and mutual support among the church members. As Marcio explained to me, peace among church members is not just encouraged; it is required:

> In the Pentecostal cells, you have to respect your brothers. You have to have good relationships with each other. You have to be willing to give what you have to others. Because in the brothers' cells, you cannot have conflict with anyone and you cannot say "I don't talk with this guy." That attitude is not an option. In the brothers' cells, everyone has to speak to each other. I have to help you. For example, we include those who are alone during visiting hour with our visitors. We might provide material help, or it might be something else, but there has to be unity.

On a practical level, peace between church members was so important because the inmates lived within a few feet of each other twenty-four hours a day. Feuding inmates could not return to their homes to cool down, and festering intermember conflicts had the potential to drastically reduce the quality of life in the cells for church members, so strife was taken seriously and dealt with immediately. According to Marcio, the biblical command to "love thy neighbor" was interpreted literally in Prison Pentecostalism.

"Unity" may be an abstract concept, but it did not remain abstract in the prison churches; in fact, it was made tangible through embodied rituals inside the cellblocks. The camaraderie and solidarity were visible in the cells—I didn't just hear about it, I saw it, and so did the other inmates.

When I attended the worship services in prison, I would often stand shoulder to shoulder with the inmates facing the pastor or song leader. I was standing in this position in Salgado during a morning worship service when the pastor took a detour from his sermon on love and told the congregation to take a few moments to tell each other, "I love you." The instructions struck me as odd, but without missing a beat, the members of the prison church and the other inmates attending the service simply turned to one another, hugged, and told each other that they loved them.

Caught off-guard, I found myself quickly engulfed in the arms of the prisoner who had been standing on my right. I wasn't expecting the hug (plus he embraced me in a way that pinned my elbows to my ribcage)—so, startled and immobilized, I was only able to utter a surprised *obrigado* (thank you). There were hundreds of hugs exchanged in the cellblocks over the next few minutes and eight or nine inmates hugged me, each saying "I love you," or "Jesus loves you." And I hugged them back.

The mid-service hugging session was not a ritual rooted in centuries of church history like communion or baptism, but it gave inmates an opportunity to act on one of the prison church's core values. In this context, love wasn't a feeling; rather, it was a command. For the Pentecostal inmates, it wasn't enough to call each other "brother." In prison, words needed to be matched by action, and unity had to be seen as well as felt.

When Pedro, the Heroes for Christ pastor, was transferred from Salgado to a prison, I saw unity embodied in a different way. During a morning worship service in Salgado, a prison guard approached the steel cellblock door and yelled down the hall. I didn't understand what the guard had said, but Pedro did. He excused himself from the worship and immediately went into his cell to grab his court documents and a white, leather-bound Bible. The men stopped singing midsong when they saw Pedro move toward the cell, and when he emerged, they surrounded him and placed their hands on his head, neck, shoulders, chest, and arms.

The church members' hands covered nearly every inch of his body, and the inmates who could not reach his body extended their hands toward Pedro's bowed head. Pedro clenched his eyes shut and squeezed his Bible while members of his church prayed for him and his upcoming meeting with the judge. Once again, an abstract concept like unity was made visible and tangible, and in his final moments inside Salgado, the support of his church literally pressed against Pedro's body. The scene also sent a powerful message to the other inmates who were observing the ritual—delivered more potently than if it had been preached in a sermon.

SHARED POSSESSIONS

Earlier in this chapter, Marcio mentioned how prison church members were expected to share resources. The prison churches I studied were independent organizations—they did not receive regular support from churches, denominations, or prison ministries. Their operating budget came from the same source as most other independent churches; they collected money from the members.

Since the jails barely provided enough material support for inmates to survive, most prisoners depended on their families or some other source to supplement basic provisions. Inmates in these facilities who did not receive visitors were in especially precarious positions because they needed to figure out how to procure basics like health care, soap, toothpaste, medicine, even clothing. If a person was arrested without a shirt, they remained shirtless until a family member or another inmate gave one to them.

After Pedro faced the judge to receive his final sentence, he was transferred to the prison to serve his time. To fill the vacancy, members of the Heroes for Christ church elected Cristiano as their new head pastor. Like many of the men in Salgado, Cristiano's family depended on his salary, which disappeared after he was arrested. "Many of us stuck in here are the providers for our families. Like me; my family depends on me." Cristiano said. He had a supportive family, but others in his church did not. "There are others who do not have anywhere to turn, and sometimes they break down and collapse, weeping bitterly, because they see that their wife needs some chicken or diapers for the children. So the church kicks in. . . . We use the tithe from church members and use it on the people who don't receive visitors. We spend it on them. We buy toothpaste, soap, prescription medicine, sandals—the basic materials to survive in here on a daily basis."

Beyond the toiletries, I saw the church "kick in" to provide emergency assistance to their fellow church members. Even though they had limited resources, I was there when the prison church bought food for an inmate's family who was not making ends meet without their dad or husband in the house and at a job. Another time, the church took a special offering and collected over 300 Reais (around US$100) to buy bus fare for an inmate's mother to travel from a neighboring state to visit him in the jail.

This aspect of prison church life is important because it shows that the church is looking after the most vulnerable and it allows the practice of generosity, which allows inmates to *be* generous people and embody their faith in concrete acts of selfless kindness.

PRAYER, PRAISE, AND PREACHING

Worship services were the center of religious life inside of prison. Like their counterparts on the streets, the Pentecostal churches inside prison held multiple worship services each week, usually four or five a week. Just over an hour long, the services were routinized into three parts: prayer, worship, and a sermon. A church member might participate in thousands of services before release.

Every service opened and closed with a communal prayer led by a prison church member. Praying inside a prison is interesting because the most obvious, pressing concern would be to ask God to get out of prison. Every inmate I spoke with told me he prayed about his sentence or an upcoming meeting with the judge, but that is not all they prayed about. The collective public prayers in the worship services expressed the core values of Prison Pentecostal theology. For example, when Pedro performed the baptismal ceremony described at the beginning of the chapter, I was allowed to record the audio on that day. I held the microphone as Pedro stood next to the freshly baptized, still-soaking men and started his prayer with words that could have been prayed in almost any Protestant church:

> We are here to give thanks to you, Lord, for this moment and for your grace. We are here as sinners; we continue to sin and we recognize that we are not worthy to be in your presence, Lord. But we thank you for this opportunity to reconcile with you, Lord, in spite of our sin.

Like most of the prayers I heard in Salgado and the other penal facilities in Rio de Janeiro, the physical and social context of the church shaped the prayers. Church members did not pretend that they were not in prison and they used prayer to show how Pentecostal theology works in the prison context. Pedro continued:

> For various reasons, our physical bodies are in this prison, but that doesn't stop us from praising you, from loving you, and from doing your will. Because our joy is not conditional. Lord, you gave us a joy that is independent of our circumstances. Even though we are physically in prison, it doesn't stop us from praising you with our lives and the work you have established in each of us.

When Pedro prayed, "Our physical bodies are in this prison but that doesn't stop us from praising you, from loving you, and from doing your will," he was capturing one of the ideas that consistently arose in my interviews with prison church members, in the songs they sang, the prayers they prayed, and the sermons they preached. One of Prison Pentecostalism's central teachings is that even though they are captives who are locked up against their will, incarcerated church members can live lives with purpose, even joy. Pedro's prayer stated that inmates, even those who had committed violent, destructive acts, could love God, praise God, and do God's will inside prison.

The prayers were not just "get me out of here," "don't let them kill me," or "forgive me for what I did." Rather, they reflected a more nuanced understanding of the faith. One of the implications of this message was that the inmates' lives were not completely defined by their incarcerated status; church members' religious identity provided an alternative framework to help them understand their place in the world. The purpose of their religious practice was not simply to survive incarceration, but to live their daily lives with dignity inside prison in a way that they felt honored God.

This paradigm was radically different than the one that predominated in larger society. This worldview was expressed, for example, by a woman interviewed as part of the research. She was asked a simple question, "What do you think about religion inside of prison?" Though she had never been in a prison, she was born and raised in Rio and had a strong opinion that captured the sentiments of other people when I asked them about the topic.

> First, I don't think that it is appropriate. Because it seems like they brainwash the people that are in there. Many of them get into this thing, Bible, Bible, Bible, some even turn into pastors. The criminals! But when they leave there, they continue to be criminals. So it is one of those things that they do to say that they have good behavior so they can get out. It isn't something they do for the rest of their lives. He is going to leave and convert others? No way. It is just . . . an act.

In her response, she hit on three themes that arose during my conversations with other noninmates over the course of the research. First is the assertion that the inmates don't really know what they are doing, implying that they do not have the analytical ability to make decisions regarding religious belief. Second, while the inmates may be sincerely religious inside of prison, they will return to their non-Pentecostal criminal ways once they are released. Finally, many of my noninmate informants said that they believed that the Pentecostal inmates were faking religious ardor in order to win favor with judges and administrators in the legal system.

These suspicions are not necessarily unreasonable; in fact, the inmates themselves were wary of jailhouse conversions, waiting and watching to see how the convert acted over time before deciding whether he was really just "hiding behind a Bible." But I contend that the promise of dignity, or living a life with purpose and meaning, not convincing outsiders, was one of the primary reasons that Prison Pentecostalism flourished in Rio's prison system.

In the last few sentences of Pedro's prayer, he touched on another crucial and familiar element of Prison Pentecostalism—personal transformation and the affirmation that God is concerned about and loves each individual prisoner:

> Father, I pray for the lives of these men today as they publicly decide to leave the world and what they have done in the past behind and become new creatures that you hold in your hands. Help them to serve you, Lord, and conform to your word in the best way they can. Help us God and hold us, your children, tightly in your hands.

I heard very few inmates claim to be innocent during the fieldwork. I have no doubt that there were completely innocent men inside the prisons and jails I studied. Many of the men I spoke to minimized their involvement in the crime they were accused of and said that the punishment they received was too harsh, but wrongful imprisonment was not a common theme in my interviews. Because most of the inmates admitted some degree of guilt and freely confessed that their pre-arrest lifestyles contributed to their current situation, the idea of change or personal transformation was central to the appeal of Prison Pentecostalism. This is why conversion or recommitment to faith was such an important part of religious practice in prison and why the church members' personal testimonies were almost always on the tips of their tongues. Baptism served as the ritualized public proclamation of personal change through religion and symbolized the experience that Pedro described in his prayer as becoming "new creatures" in the eyes of God.

Finally, Pedro's prayer reflected how Prison Pentecostals perceive the Christian God—as a supernatural being who is intimately involved in the lives of the inmates. Pedro prayed, "Help us, God, and hold us, your children, tightly in your hands." The image presented by Pedro and repeated over and over in the worship services was that God interacted with humans, including convicted criminals, like a caring parent.

God as an all-loving, all-forgiving father is an abstract concept that was embodied through the deeply emotional religious practice in the cellblocks. Just over a week before the baptism ceremony, three volunteers from the local Deus é Amor (God Is Love) church came to Salgado to host the weekly worship service inside the Comando Vermelho cellblock. The Pentecostal volunteers were all members of the same family—two parents in their mid-fifties and their daughter, who was probably close to thirty. In the sermon delivered by the soft-spoken mother, she told the men that their lives were in God's hands, but sensing that her words were not resonating with the gang members, she stopped the sermon and told them, "Just for a moment forget your troubles, forget your worries, and forget all of the things that you have to resolve today. Close your eyes and remember that your help is in Jesus—look to Jesus."

She then instructed everyone participating in the service to close his eyes, place the palm of one hand on the side of his face, and embrace himself with his other arm. Once her audience's eyes were closed and arms wrapped in self-embrace, the woman told the men to imagine that it was Jesus who was holding them. She told them, "Imagine Jesus is holding you right now. Let Jesus talk to you right now." The service was held in the space controlled by the CV, and though there was not a prison church operating in the gang's cells, all of the radios and televisions were muted during this time, and no one spoke. All twenty gang members attending the service stood in the instructed position, closed their eyes, and participated in the ritual that aimed to portray Jesus as a supernatural being who loved each person and was intimately concerned with their spiritual and physical lives.

I have no way to know what was "really" going on in the heads of the participants. Some remained stoic; others prayed softly and others wept quietly. It was clearly a meaningful exercise for some of the inmates, but it was also an example of how core principles of the faith are brought down to earth from the realm of the abstract and cerebral and made visible and embodied in very difficult circumstances. It is also important to recall at this point that gang members are among the most reviled citizens of Rio de Janeiro—they are the city's killable people. The purpose of the ritual was to confront this stigma and convey to these men that they are viewed differently in Jesus' eyes. The Pentecostal volunteer's hope was that embodying this message would reach the inmates in a way that simply telling them would not.

WORSHIP

The music never stopped inside prison. Radios and CD players blared throughout the day in the cellblocks. When the volume was turned down to accommodate the worship services, inmates sang praise songs a capella or accompanied by a tambourine, and the clapping of hands replaced the heavier beats from the radios. After studying Pentecostalism throughout the global South, Donald Miller and Tetsunao Yamamori (2007, 23–24) concluded, "The engine of Pentecostalism is its worship . . . the heart of Pentecostalism is the music. It touches the emotions. It is populist in tone and instrumentation. And the lyrics give voice to feelings—the pain, the joy, the hope for a new life." Their conclusion mirrored what I observed inside the prisons and jails in Rio de Janeiro.

Before I started the fieldwork, I assumed that the most important part of the worship service would be the sermon. This reflected my own bias and familiarity with non-Pentecostal Protestant services in North America. I quickly learned that my assumption was wrong; in the prison services, the worship was more than the appetizer for the sermon—it was the meat and potatoes or, in this case, the rice and beans of the meal.

During the worship service, inmates in both the prisons and jails pulled songs from the Pentecostal canon of music that is played in churches throughout the country. Some were translated classics like "Old Rugged Cross," but most were Brazilian originals that could be heard in any of the thousands of Pentecostal churches throughout the country. Though none of the songs the inmates sung were written specifically for the prison context, when inmates sang them inside of prison, the songs underwent a contextual reinterpretation.

One song that was particularly conducive to this sort of reinterpretation was "Advogado Fiel," or "Faithful Lawyer," which was released on an album nominated for a Latino Grammy in 2010 under the "Best Christian Album" category:

> *I will not worry about persecution*
> *With the stones they throw at me, Jesus is near*
> *I can trust, I can rest, Jesus is near*
>
> *Who casts the first stone? It is he who is without sin, he who*
>   *makes no mistakes*
> *To defend me before the enemy*
> *Take my pain, to cry with me*
> *To support me under Thy right hand, this is an unmitigated fact,*
> *My impossible cases will always be closed by my lawyer.*
>
> *My lawyer is my Lord*
> *He defends me against the accuser*
> *I put my cause in his hands*
> *He has already marked my hearing*
> *And once again assured that I will be the winner*
> *My lawyer lives in the heaven*
> *True, fair, forever faithful*
>
> *Faithful lawyer, faithful lawyer*
> *That is what my Jesus is for me*

Faithful lawyer, faithful lawyer
That is what my Jesus is for me

The song was not written specifically for the 500,000 incarcerated Brazilians—in fact it was released by an attractive young Christian pop star, Bruna Karla, in her early twenties. But inside prison, the song was sung as a literal prayer. Prisoners made the song their own by rooting it in their own context.

Few of the inmates in the jail could afford to hire private lawyers and from their perspective, the criminal justice process was marked by uncertainty and distrust. Some of the men had been in jail awaiting trial for over a year, and the anticipation left them exhausted and frustrated. I saw jailed inmates who were waiting for their trial or waiting to receive their sentence hold their court documents in outstretched hands as they sang the chorus of the song: "My lawyer is my Lord, he defends me against the accuser. My faithful lawyer, my faithful lawyer that is what Jesus is to me."

Andrew Chesnut (1997) argued that Pentecostalism flourished in the Amazonian capital of Belém because it presented a response to a tangible problem—sickness—in a place where formal healthcare was unavailable to the poor. He argued that those who were sick and had little access to doctors or hospitals were attracted to the Pentecostal faith because it offered supernatural, though not scientifically proven, remedies for their ailments. As I cited earlier in the book, 90 percent of respondents in Chesnut's study of Pentecostalism in Belém identified supernatural healing as a reason they converted to the faith. For the detainees awaiting their upcoming trials inside Rio's jails, Pentecostalism offered an analogous appeal—a supernatural response to their earthly crisis.

Like the collective prayers, songs like "Faithful Lawyer" served to teach and reinforce central components of Prison Pentecostal theology. The line "Who casts the first stone? It is he who is without sin, he who makes no mistakes," a quotation from Jesus in the New Testament book of John, is an example of Jesus aligning himself with the accused, not the accuser. The prisons and jails of Rio de

Janeiro are located in a very different social, cultural, and historical context than first-century Samaria, but Jesus' actions toward the women he met at the well resonated powerfully with inmates who were facing their own accusers. According to the religious law at the time, the woman deserved to die for the wrong she had done, but Jesus stepped in and confronted the accusers with the wrongdoing in their own lives.

SERMONS

Decades ago, my dad volunteered at a mission that served hot meals and provided temporary shelter for men living on what served as "Skid Row" in Minneapolis, Minnesota. When church groups volunteered at the mission, a visiting pastor gave a brief sermon from a wooden pulpit to the men before they received their food. When the pastor arrived at the pulpit he or she was greeted with a note placed by the mission's staff: "Please do not preach on the prodigal son. Thank you." The message was written to let the visiting preacher know that they were not the first one to recognize the parallels between the biblical story and the men at the mission; it was a polite way of saying, "They have heard that one already."

Personal transformation was the most common theme preached during the worship service sermons, and "once was I lost, but now I am found" testimonies delivered from inmates to their peers provided credibility to the promise of change. The sermons were not only calls for repentance and conversion. In most cases, the audience listening to the sermons had already converted, and the inmate pastors focused their message instead on deepening the faith of their congregation and on how God can use the lives of the inmates to impact those around them, both inside prison and after their release.

Cristiano gave this type of sermon when he walked to the front of the Heroes for Christ congregation in Salgado. He started his sermon by reading from the creation account in Genesis, building on the phrase "let there be light" and concluded with the following:

> When the word says, "let there be light," it means that there will be an incredible transformation in a place where no one believed there could be change. When many people look at you, they see a person without form, empty, and trembling in the abyss.
>
> They don't believe that you can change into something beautiful. Because their predetermined vision teaches them to believe that we are something we are not.
>
> But I want to say one thing to you. It only takes one word from God to change your life.
>
> God believes that you can be transformed!
>
> God has a word of victory for you today—God wants to transform your life!
>
> He wants to transform this difficult moment into a moment of victory!
>
> When you leave here and go back to society again, you will be a rich source of transformation and wisdom. You will not only change your own lives, but you will change the lives of people close to you.
>
> Let there be light in your life today, my brother. In the name of Jesus, let there be light in your life.

Cristiano knew that he was speaking to a group of men of whom the majority had converted or recommitted to Christianity inside of prison. So while he continued to preach about personal transformation, he told his fellow inmates that they could be light, or a transforming force for their families and friends outside of prison. They did not just need to be transformed; they could be used by God to transform others close to them.

Cristiano was telling the inmates that their Prison Pentecostalism was legitimate in any context, not just inside the cellblock in Salgado Jail. His message was very different from the skepticism of many observers on the outside who think that inmates use religion for some temporary instrumental purpose. To Cristiano, not only were the members of his church not "hiding behind a Bible," but they had something to teach nonprisoners about the power of faith.

Cristiano's paradigm reversal resonated with his audience. I could see this connection as the men nodded their heads, shouted *alleluia*, and applauded as Cristiano reached his conclusion. It was an empowering message because it affirmed the dignity of the inmates' lives by pushing back against the notion that their faith was insincere and their destiny was simply to be one of Rio's killable people.

FAITH IN ACTION

For inmates, simply saying "I believe" wasn't enough to convince others in prison of their religious convictions. Words alone wouldn't persuade people on the outside either. An inmate's daily actions had to align with his stated religious affiliation, which demanded a high degree of personal discipline on the part of the believer. Because the inmates in Rio's prisons elevated practice over self-reported belief when assessing an inmate's devotion to prison religion, I followed their lead and implemented a lived religion perspective in the research. I focused primarily on the rituals, experiences, and emotions of the religious men in prison and less intently on their belief systems. Determining whether Pentecostal inmates *really* believed may be a legitimate question, but it is outside the bounds of my research. It wasn't the inmates' grasp of theology that was tested while they were in prison; it was whether their lives reflected a true change of heart.

The rigorous practice demanded by Prison Pentecostalism probably deterred some inmates who may have been interested in the faith, but they were intimidated or put off by the prison churches' strict requirements. Rio's prison churches did not follow the "seeker sensitive" model for church growth, but instead set the membership bar high. That was one of the reasons the faith thrived inside prison.

First, being high-commitment churches allowed the Pentecostal groups inside of Rio's prisons and jails to represent a united front to other inmates, especially the gangs. Hearing the worship songs that rang throughout the cellblocks and seeing the church members publicly pray for each other showed the other inmates, especially gang leaders, that the prison church was a cohesive and unified group even if it represented less than 10 percent of the prison population.

Another way the emphasis on daily, visible practice helped prison churches thrive was that the rituals, worship services, and tithing and fasting campaigns provided a way for inmates to *be* different people. When I first started the research, I thought that having four or five worship services a week was overkill—imagine going to 250 worship services a year! But as I continued the fieldwork inside of the prison, I changed my perspective. I started to see that participating in these services gives inmates a chance to "prove" that they were serious about their vocalized religious commitments. Also, the catharsis many men experienced during the worship services needed to be repeated consistently in order to effect real transformation—part of the "one day at a time" strategy that many inmates used to survive their prison sentences.

The rituals, whether singing, tithing, or hugging, not only sent a message of love and unity to the onlookers, but also were part of the transformation process so integral to Prison Pentecostalism. The daily practice gave opportunities for inmates to act upon their stated religious commitments and become the generous, self-sacrificing, loving people their faith demanded while they were still incarcerated.

Repeatedly participating in these activities changed the dispositions of some of the inmates and also changed how they saw themselves. The practices allowed them to *be* transformed people and embody their religious conversion. For example, when Junho started to read his Bible every day after his prison conversion, he reported a change in his life. The way Junho described it, the difference he experienced wasn't due entirely to the content of the passages he was reading; rather, it was the fact that he was reading the Bible every day as part of his newfound discipline and devotion. He was following through on a commitment and making different choices, from not doing drugs to participating in religious rituals every day. These choices not only changed the way others saw him—they also served as both evidence of and fuel for the transformation of his life as he understood it. Which is why a few weeks after he converted, Junho said, "Man, I'd never seen myself like this before. I started to see that I was different, and when my mother came to visit, even she saw that I was different."

By employing a lived religion perspective, I do not mean to imply that theology was not an important part of the success of Prison Pentecostalism. In fact, focusing on the inmates' daily practice provided an avenue to gather data and understand Prison Pentecostal theology in greater detail. The prison churches shared core theological principles with the Pentecostal churches outside of prison, but the prison context shaped the particular theology of these churches. Debates over theological nuances that have divided and separated Pentecostal congregations since the Azusa Street Revival were not present in the prison churches I studied. I never observed or heard of prison church schisms, nor did I hear inmate pastors identify themselves based on abstract theological markers like premillennial, postmillennial, Calvinist, or Armenian. More importantly, given that the prison churches were Pentecostal, it was surprising that there was not any requirement to speak in tongues or have any particular manifestations of the Holy Spirit to confirm a conversion or affiliation with the church. Some form of these manifestations is usually the hallmark of Pentecostal experience in noninmate Pentecostal churches.

A persistent theological theme that I did observe in the prison churches' preaching, singing, and daily life was the idea of dignity. The message from the prison church to the members and the rest of the congregation was clear: Your life has value despite your current incarceration. It was a countercultural message that pushed back against the dominant narrative that the inmates' lives were worthless. Prison Pentecostal preaching and teaching did not argue that prisoners were innocent, but it rejected the idea that they are killable by using a different paradigm to measure individual self-worth. The inmates may have been guilty under the law and hated by society, but they were forgiven by God and loved by each other.

Many of the men I spoke with were proud of the lives they were living inside prison and proud of the church they belonged to. The fact that the prison churches were independent, self-sustaining organizations contributed to the dignity of the members. Prison church members were not the objects of charity or subject to the whims of outsiders deciding the direction of their church.

When I first attended a service at the Cinza Penitentiary church, I was surprised that the church's worship band used electric guitars and a bass, an expensive drum kit, and an excellent sound system. The church had purchased these instruments with tithes collected from the inmate church members. If I am completely honest, I have to confess that I silently wondered if that was the best way to spend the money, given the dire material needs that many of the members' families were experiencing. But I came to realize that the instruments served a purpose that was larger and more important than providing music for the worship songs and amplifying the sermon so that it could be heard throughout the entire prison. The instruments symbolized what the inmates had accomplished in their church. Even though they were among their city's most stigmatized residents, they had built a church where they experienced joy, brotherhood, and dignity in one of Rio's most apparently god-forsaken places.

CHAPTER 6

THE POLITICS
OF PRESENCE

Shortly before noon on Monday, November 9, 2010, authorities lost
control of the Pedrinhas Prison Complex in São Luis, capital of the
northeastern Brazilian state of Maranhão. A rivalry that had been
simmering for weeks between factions of prisoners from two different
regions boiled over into a riot. More than a dozen inmates were killed,
and law enforcement officials were sent to collect three prisoners' sev-
ered heads that had been thrown over the prison walls. Inside the facility, corpses were piled in a janitor's closet, five prison employees had
been taken hostage, and the rioters marked five more inmates for execution if the rioters' demands were not met. São Luis's police commis-
sioner, Daniel Brandão, needed to act swiftly but did not want to send
in the military police because that would certainly double or triple
the casualties. Brandão made a decision that has become increasingly
common for prison officials facing this type of situation in Brazil: He
called on a Pentecostal pastor to negotiate a truce.

Marcos Pereira, a minister for the Last Days Assemblies of God
(LDAG) church in one of the gritty neighborhoods on the periphery
of Rio de Janeiro, received the call from the prison marshal that afternoon. The rioting inmates, fearful of being slaughtered if the military
police invaded the prison, had asked for Pastor Marcos to mediate the
situation. Within a couple of hours, the pastor and ten other church
members had boarded a plane to São Luis, a city nearly two thousand
miles north of their church. The group arrived at midnight and went
straight to the prison, which was by now completely under inmate
control. Pastor Pereira spoke with inmate leaders through a cellphone

143

that had been smuggled inside and agreed to return the next morning to start negotiations.

On November 10, Pastor Pereira and the church members were allowed to enter the prison complex, passing through the lines of heavily armed police officers. The Pentecostal group walked across the prison yard to the cellblocks, where the pastor spoke to the inmates through barred windows. After several tense moments (filmed by a church member with a handheld camera) the door opened and two hostages emerged unharmed. The remaining three hostages were freed an hour later.

Pereira then entered the building to speak with the riot leaders and emerged in less than an hour with three handguns and a collection of knives that they had surrendered. The siege was over. Immediately after the pastor turned over the weapons to the prison officials, the LDAG team gathered the inmates in the prison's patio and held a worship service with them. The LDAG volunteers sang praise songs and prayed over the inmates as the prison officials removed the cadavers from the corridor and started to clean floors and walls that were still wet with blood.

A POLITICS OF PRESENCE

At first glance, Pastor Marcos's intervention in the Pedrinhas prison riot fit the long-standing critique of Brazilian Pentecostal interaction with larger society: They focus on the individual or temporary crisis, while ignoring the root structural causes of suffering and inequality. Though most interactions I observed between pastors and prisons were not as dramatic as Marcos's successful intervention in the Pedrinhas riot, for the most part Pentecostals primarily focused their efforts on convincing individual inmates to turn from their lives of crime and submit themselves, body and soul, to God. For example, Pastor Marcos arrived with members from his church and helped to negotiate a temporary peace between the inmates and the state, but once the riot was over, the group from LDAG returned to their church, never challenging the underlying issues that caused the riot. LDAG did not organize church members in an effort to transform the prison system by writing letters to local politicians or holding public protests to push for prison reform.

There is no doubt that the Pentecostals I observed and spoke with in this study emphasized working with individual inmates and prisons over traditional political or social movement action. But I think the dichotomy that places religious actors into one of two camps—those concerned with the lives of individuals and those concerned with reforming social structures and institutions—is a false one. The Pentecostals choose to enter prisons on a daily basis, step into the middle of crisis events, and muster resources to meet the material needs of inmates—a choice that is mistakenly characterized as the driver of an apolitical movement whose ground troops, often from the same *favelas* as the inmates, are somehow oblivious to the structural inequalities that produce Rio's abysmal prison system.

In Rio de Janeiro, rather than voting for a particular candidate, aligning with a party, or pushing for specific legislation, Pentecostal pastors and volunteers choose to stand shoulder-to-shoulder with the prisoners. Their choice to *be there* reflects the kind of vision and many of the goals that grassroots social movements typically pursue. Pentecostal pastors raised awareness about Rio's prisons by reporting back to their congregations and imploring members to become involved in the lives of the city's inmates. In addition, their presence in prison delivered a countercultural message. Through their actions the Pentecostal pastors and volunteers literally embodied their belief that regardless of whether the inmates in Rio's prisons were innocent or guilty of the crimes of which they were convicted, they were human beings worthy of redemption and deserving certain fundamental rights. They pushed back against the idea that inmates were killable people. Moreover, they affirmed the essential dignity of all the inmates by devoting time and resources to them, building on the message preached by the inmate-led prison churches.

I WAS IN PRISON AND YOU CAME
TO VISIT ME

Prisons are places from which people are generally trying to leave. But one of the problems many jail administrators face is the overwhelming number of Pentecostal pastors and volunteers who want to visit Rio's prisons. Any time I visited a prison or jail, Pentecostal pastors and volunteers were queued outside of the facility. During my time in Salgado, a dozen churches (Pastor Marcos's included) made weekly visits to the cellblocks to hold worship services and sometimes provide first-aid material like bandages, disinfectant, and basic medicines. The jail's warden complained to me that in his previous post, he had to deal with seventeen Pentecostal churches making weekly visits to his relatively small jail. He said that trying to schedule all of them was a major part of his job—and a logistical headache.

Still, the Pentecostal pastors and volunteers who visited the prisons, and whose benign familiarity with both inmates and guards meant that they were sometimes called upon to be peacemakers, rarely described their actions as politically motivated. In fact, when asked about their motivations, they gave theological responses that situate them squarely within the emergent Progressive Pentecostal movement in the developing world. Miller and Yamamori (2007) identified this movement as "Christians who claim to be inspired by the Holy Spirit and the life of Jesus and who seek to holistically address the spiritual, physical, and social needs of people in their community" (212). In other words, Progressive Pentecostals are not concerned with only saving souls and resisting the temptations of this world; they are on the front lines of efforts to address the social consequences of poverty, violence, drug addiction, and a host of other problems.

For example, in the jails, there were absolutely no medical services offered by the state; all of the medical supplies were brought in by inmates' family members or donated by a religious group or individual. Many families had depended on the income, often illegal, that abruptly stopped when their son, brother, or father was incarcerated.

In response to this acute need, some of the pastors operated church-based ministries that provided assistance to the prisoners' families.

I accompanied a number of pastors who visited inmates' families all across the city, bringing boxes of food, consoling words, and messages from the prisoner to their spouse, child, or parents. Inmates were keenly aware of where the medical supplies came from. And they knew who visited their families, as well as the families of their cellmates, to provide comfort and assistance. Miller and Yamamori (2007) argue that this form of stabilizing social engagement is one of the reasons Pentecostalism has grown so quickly in Latin America. I would add that it is also one of the primary reasons that the faith has become so deeply rooted in Rio's prison life.

RESPONDING TO VIOLENCE IN RIO'S PRISONS

One way to measure the scope of the Pentecostals' social engagement—which I describe as a "politics of presence"—is to closely examine their interventions in violent or potentially violent situations in prisons. Beyond the bloody riots that periodically grabbed headlines, inmates routinely murdered other inmates, guards killed and were killed, and there was little political will to change the situation among the general populace. This civic apathy on the part of Rio's more affluent citizens allowed institutional corruption and violence to saturate the entire penal system.

The most common way pastors responded to the suffering generated by this malign neglect was by defending inmates who were facing the threat of imminent harm from other prisoners. Marcelo,[1] an inmate in his early twenties, was thrown into Salgado with bruises on his face, arms, and torso that he had acquired during his arrest. When I met Marcelo I also noticed the poorly planned tattoos that covered his shoulders and the very anxious look in his bloodshot eyes. Days after he was arrested, he was still shirtless, with a tiny photo of his daughter hanging from his neck by a piece of string. The photo was set in a frame that was fashioned out of metallic candy wrappers. It was heartbreaking to see the smiling face of that four-year-old girl gazing out at the dismal, dungeonlike conditions of Salgado. Over the next six months, I never saw Marcelo without his daughter's photo around his neck, and when he prayed during the worship services, he held the photo between the thumbs of his folded hands and pressed it against his lips as he spoke his prayers.

Marcelo had many reasons to pray. Rio police officers had cornered Marcelo and three colleagues during an armed-robbery attempt. In the shootout that ensued, one of the members of the crew shot and killed a police officer. Since Marcelo was the only member of the crew who had been captured, he sat in jail awaiting trial for the murder of a police officer. One afternoon, a group of four police officers arrived at the jail and informed the warden they had orders to transfer Marcelo to another facility. The officers had showed up at an odd time of day, and they didn't have an official transport vehicle, so when word reached the cellblocks, Marcelo panicked. He knew instantly that the officers had come to kill him.

While the police officers were speaking to the warden, Pastor Cicero—the leader of a storefront church in a poor neighborhood—was leading worship songs inside the Comando Vermelho section of the cellblock. He was in the middle of a passionate chorus when Marcelo interrupted the pastor and pulled him aside. Marcelo told the pastor about the men who had arrived to "transfer" him, and he begged Pastor Cicero to intervene. After listening to Marcelo's pleas and receiving confirmation of his story from other inmates, Pastor Cicero abruptly ended the service, asked to be let out of the cells, and went directly to the warden.

"Please don't do this, warden," he begged. "In the name of Jesus, don't give this man to them."

The police officers eventually left the jail empty-handed, and Marcelo stayed in his cell. It is impossible to know exactly what convinced the warden to refuse the officers' request. Pastor Cicero told me that Marcelo was spared because "God touched the warden's heart at that moment." When I talked to Marcelo, he told me the pastor had saved his life.

Moreover, the pastor's stabilizing and consistent presence in the jail allowed him to alter the way the warden, a cog in the machinery of a corrupt state, used his power over inmates' lives.

Still, Pastor Cicero's intervention reflected a Pentecostal theology that focuses on the individual who is suffering rather than the larger social problems that cause him or her to suffer. Pastor Cicero did not set his sights on "saving" the prison system. In fact, he didn't report the incident to the press or even make a formal complaint. Instead he focused on meeting the needs of individual prisoners. He would leave it to others to decide whether and how to reform a penal system that countenanced off-duty police officers showing up at a jail to execute a man accused of killing a cop.

The paradox of Progressive Pentecostalism is that even if faith-based activists like Pastor Cicero claim no concern for changing the institutional structures that deepen poverty and exacerbate violence at Rio's social margins, their activism nonetheless alters those structures. To illustrate the process, this chapter will examine the implications of Pentecostal action, like Pastor Cicero's intervention, beyond saving the life of Marcelo.

BLESSED ARE THE PEACEMAKERS

Not all Pentecostal responses to violence in prison focus solely on individual inmates; in fact, some of their interventions engage entire prisons. This chapter opened with a description of a prison riot that was quelled by Pastor Marcos Pereira and the members of the Last Days Assemblies of God, a church that has been involved in mediating truces in a dozen prison riots.

Pastor Marcos was a tireless self-promoter and spoke frequently about his peacemaking skills during interviews and his sermons at LDAG. A few years ago, church members started to bring video cameras with them wherever they went. They published the clips and images through various media outlets. DVDs of Pastor Marcos's "greatest hits" were for sale at more than a dozen informal markets throughout the city and helped to elevate him to celebrity status in Rio's *favelas*. Though the images in these DVDs (many recorded in prison) were powerful, they were also a not-so-subtle component of his church's propaganda campaign and presented a very one-sided version of events.

To get another perspective on the pastor's work mediating prison riots, I interviewed ex-inmates who were incarcerated during these uprisings. Junho, the Comando Vermelho member who was put on trial by his gang, was an inmate in Rio's most infamous maximum-security prison when a riot that broke out after several key gang-affiliated inmates were transferred to another facility. The remaining portion of the gang hierarchy demanded that all inmates in gang-controlled cellblocks throw their mattresses into the hallways and set them on fire. The riot escalated very quickly, and from Junho's perspective, the pastor's arrival was a divine intervention in a situation that had gotten out of control:

> I don't know what hell is really like, but I'll tell you that things were really ugly there. The [gang leader] in charge of the prison ordered people to set fire to the mattresses and everything. They made a huge bonfire, and the prison doesn't have any ventilation system—it's just a big passage without any outlet for the smoke, so the smoke from the mattresses began to fall down, and there wasn't any ventilation system. The smoke kept falling and it looked like the roof was caving in with all of that smoke. People were dying from suffocation and people were being trampled. The riot squad arrived, wanting to get in, wanting to get in, and I remember it as if it was today. The only person who was able to get inside to calm the prisoners was Pastor Marcos. If the riot squad had come in they would have killed everyone, you know? ... If the riot squad had gotten in that day, I would be dead, man.

Junho's account of the prison riot and its resolution reveals how pastors' interventions often rely on charismatic authority, what Max Weber (1968) described as "a certain quality of an individual personality by virtue of which he is considered extraordinary and treated as endowed with supernatural, superhuman, or at least specifically exceptional powers or qualities" (241). A pastor's ability to respond effectively to violence hinged on his or her identity as a man or woman of God; in other words, it depended on the pastor's charisma.

I asked Junho why the active gang members in the prison were so responsive to Pastor Marcos, given that they were not professing Pentecostals. Junho's response emphasized the importance of visible displays of divine power: "Pastor Marcos came in with signs and wonders, so the inmates respected him. Pastor Marcos arrived, came into the building, and started freeing people from the demons that were in the prison. He prayed during the riot and on that day the riot ended."

When Pastor Marcos "freed" an inmate from his demons, he placed his hands on the inmate's head and prayed for him until the inmate fell to the floor, seemingly unconscious and "slain in the spirit." I saw the LDAG team facilitate many worship services in Salgado as well as at street revivals in Comando Vermelho territory outside the prison. Almost all of the services ended with this sort of charismatic prayer. During one service inside Salgado, the LDAG members started praying for the inmates in the cellblocks and within ten minutes, there were over a dozen inmates lying motionless on the jail floor. When the church members finished praying, I was the only person left standing within a ten-foot radius. I literally could not take a step from my spot because the bodies of dozens of "slain" inmates took up all the space on the floor of the cellblock.

Many outsiders are skeptical of this sort of prayer and its effects, including some Pentecostals, who have accused Pastor Marcos of employing a form of hypnosis.[2] To be honest, I was not sure what exactly was happening when I saw inmates slump to the floor at the end of the prayer; I can say with fair certainty that they were not faking unconsciousness. In any case, determining what was "really" going on during these prayers lies beyond the scope of this project. I am also certain that Pastor Marcos's visible display of power resonated with some of the inmates. This sort of power contributed to the charismatic authority that Pentecostal pastors held in prison and it was essential to the influence they were able to exert among all the inmates.

A PASTOR'S PROTEST

Some pastors' responses to prison violence went beyond protecting individual inmates or even entire prison populations from immediate danger, and they used this broader influence to pressure the state to improve living conditions in penal institutions. Antonio Carlos Costa, a Presbyterian pastor and president of Rio de Paz, was one example. He implored not only inmates to surrender their souls to the Lord, but also the state to reform the prisons that housed those inmates. Antonio stood out from most of the pastors visiting prisons and jails in Rio de Janeiro because his congregation was largely middle- and upper-class. He was one of the few "non-Pentecostal" Protestant pastors I met who was regularly active in the prison system. The inmates were indifferent to this denominational distinction and bestowed on Costa the same title as Pentecostal ministers: "Pastor."

Pastor Antonio visited the prison every two weeks and brought a team of dentists, nurses, and volunteers from his church to provide basic medical care to the inmates before and after the worship services. It was a larger, more tightly organized project than the undertakings of the storefront churches, but the worship services led by Costa and his team employed the same key features: singing, preaching, and an invitation for inmates to make personal commitments to God.

Pastor Antonio and the volunteers from Rio de Paz could respond to the inmates' spiritual and medical needs, but addressing the problem of astonishingly overcrowded cells was more complicated. As I described earlier in the book, in Salgado, generally two inmates would sleep head-to-toe on narrow, concrete bunkbeds and detainees who couldn't score a bunk would simply curl up on the concrete floor. A few paid a daily fee to cell leaders to spend a few hours or entire days in an ad hoc hammock system, but no matter what sleeping innovations were implemented, there simply was not enough space to hold all the bodies. Some inmates remained standing for much of the night, waiting their turn to squeeze into one of the spaces, or tying themselves to the cell's bars with t-shirts in an attempt to sleep in a vertical position.

Pastor Antonio was appalled by this situation and had unsuccessfully petitioned the city government to address the problem. When we were in one of Salgado's cells together, the pastor pointed to the dozens of sweating bodies crammed into a very small cell and said, "This is illegal. We don't need new legislation to change this; we need to enforce the laws we already have."

After months of stalling and unsatisfactory answers from city police officials, Pastor Antonio called on volunteers from his church and Rio de Paz to start building a structure the exact size of a Salgado jail cell in the middle of Copacabana Beach, one of the city's most iconic and tourist-heavy spaces. He said he would then fill the replica of the jail cell with seventy volunteers (the number of inmates that occupied the real cell) so that reporters, journalists, wealthier local beachgoers, and tourists could see what one of Rio's "overcrowded prisons" really looks like—a stark contrast to the image that the city had promoted in its winning bids for the 2014 World Cup and the 2016 Olympic Games.

When they were informed of Pastor Antonio's intentions, police officials became much more attentive to his pleas. A high-ranking member of the department soon offered to transfer a significant number of inmates from Salgado to reduce the number of inmates in each cell. The municipal government promised action by a certain date, and in return, asked for assurances that Pastor Antonio would not create the public display. The city officials kept their word, and the inmates were transferred. While the pastor's threat was not the only reason the local civil authorities acted, it was a key variable in the city's equation. The pastor's regular and benign presence in the jail provided the platform for the potential protest. That presence gave him credibility with the inmates, a firsthand understanding of the horrible conditions in the prisons and a way to leverage his position in order to nudge a neglectful government into at least appearing to mend its ways.

Antonio Costa had what I call a "connected charisma." The inmates regarded him as a pastor and treated him with the corresponding reverence, but also he had a series of important connections in the government and business world through the prosperous and well-connected members of his congregation and neighborhood. He used the charismatic authority granted to him by the prison population, but his relationships with people of influence, including members of the local and international media, allowed him to pressure the state to act on his demands. Very few of the pastors I met had these kinds of social connections in their toolkit, but they were essential to Pastor Antonio's ability to parlay his charismatic authority into a successful strategy to pressure the Salgado administration to address its prison problems in a humane way.

A CLOSE CALL

My cellphone buzzed one afternoon with an incoming call from an unknown number. When I answered I immediately recognized the voice of Lucas, the leader of the CV cells in Salgado. Two weeks earlier, he had escaped from Salgado along with a dozen other incarcerated gang members. I had gotten to know Lucas well during my research, so I was concerned when I saw his photo in the newspaper next to the article detailing the escape and warning the public about the fugitives now hiding out in the city.

I asked Lucas how he was doing, hoping that he wasn't going to ask to spend a night or two on my couch. He didn't ask anything of me—he said he called "just to let you know that I am safe and everything is alright. I am with God and with my family. I am cool."

We spoke for three or four minutes, and I ended our conversation by offering to call a pastor we both knew. The idea sounded good to him, and we agreed to speak again in the next day or two. I knew Lucas's situation was not sustainable, and my immediate concern was that if the police found him, he might not survive the arrest.

I spoke to our mutual acquaintance, the pastor, the next day. We discussed the risks and logistics of arranging a face-to-face meeting with Lucas. The pastor called a trusted source at the police department and told him that he was in contact with a fugitive. Without revealing any specifics of the situation, he inquired about the legality of communicating with the man. The police official informed him that he could meet with the fugitive as long as it was in a public setting and not in a private residence or gang-controlled *favela*. He emphasized that the pastor could not give the fugitive any money or financial assistance and implored him to be careful. The pastor then asked if the police department could guarantee the safety of the individual if he agreed to surrender. The pastor's friend gave his word that he could guarantee a safe surrender and safe passage up to the prison door but said he could not guarantee anything after that.

The pastor thanked his friend at the police department and hung up the phone, and then we discussed the options. He contacted a lawyer from his church, who reluctantly agreed to sit down with the fugitive, look over his case, and explain his options. The pastor was concerned that his phone was being monitored by the government—a common concern in Rio among pastors working in the prisons or with gang members. So we used mine instead. The two men spoke for twenty minutes and Lucas confessed that he was stuck. He was in the middle of a turn toward a commitment to Pentecostal Christianity but had not formally left the gang. Not all conversion experiences happened in an instant. The CV had arranged the escape through a series of bribes, and Lucas said that if he hadn't crawled through the hole in the ceiling to escape he would have faced serious repercussions from CV members inside the jail.

Once outside of the prison and on the lam, he didn't want to return to serving the CV, and he did not want to return to prison—the prospect of serving the eight years that remained on his sentence seemed too much to bear. The pastor did not have any concrete advice for Lucas, but he told the fugitive in no uncertain terms that he as a pastor did not have the moral authority to say whether Lucas *should* turn himself in. They both knew the conditions inside the prison and understood the consequences Lucas might face on the inside. He told Lucas two other things that Lucas already knew—he was in danger and he couldn't hide forever. Lucas thanked the pastor for his concern and the time for a meeting was set.

I met Lucas the next day at one of the busiest intersections in downtown Rio. He was an hour late for the meeting, and I was ready to give up on the whole idea when I felt a tug on the back of my shirt. Lucas was wearing a soccer jersey and a matching cap worn low to cover his face. We had arranged to meet the pastor and the lawyer at a restaurant located on the first floor of one of the busiest office buildings in the city. When we arrived, Lucas and the pastor embraced like old friends. The lawyer, visibly uncomfortable, broke the ice by making a playfully disparaging comment about Lucas's soccer jersey, which belonged to a rival team.

While the restaurant's host led us to our table, I recognized a man sitting by himself eating lunch and reading a book ten feet from our table. I couldn't place his face initially, but when I did, my heart started to pump hard and fast. I grabbed the pastor by the shoulder and told him not to look right now, but a mutual acquaintance was sitting at the next table—a high-ranking police official whom we each knew.

We took our seats and when the pastor looked over his shoulder and saw the man in question, the color drained from his face and his lower lip dropped an inch. The pastor knew the police official much better than I did. He looked at me and whispered urgently, "We have to go." Looking back, it was unlikely that the police official would have recognized Lucas, but that was a chance no one at our table wanted to take. I tapped Lucas on the arm and whispered to the lawyer that we had to get out and get out fast. The three of us set our menus down and started to head for the door as the server looked on, completely bewildered at our hasty exit.

The lawyer left the restaurant like he was shot from a cannon. Lucas and I followed him with our eyes pointed toward the floor and with purpose in our stride. As we were weaving through the tables toward the exit, the pastor stood up, turned around, and called out the name of the police official. He walked toward him, arms extended for an embrace, and when he arrived at the table, he hugged the police official in a way that provided cover for the three of us bolting toward the door.

Lucas, the pastor, the lawyer, and I rendezvoused in the back of a café across the street. All of us still rattled, we traded "Can you believe what just happened" expressions across the table where we sat. The pastor said the police official didn't pick up on our dramatic exit and we all exhaled and shook our heads at the close call. We proceeded to look over Lucas's court documents, and the pastor told Lucas that if he wanted to turn himself in, he would bring a group from his church to walk with Lucas to the door of the prison to send a message to the guards and administration that there were people on the outside who were concerned for his safety. Lucas thanked us and said he would think about what he would do. He then lowered his hat another inch and melted back into the crowded streets.

Lucas didn't turn himself into the police and never had a chance to get the promised escort to the prison door. He was arrested a few months after our meeting, and the last I heard, he was serving the rest of his sentence. The scene at the restaurant illustrated two important themes in pastors' involvement in violent or potentially violent situations with inmates. First, pastors can use their respected position in prison to protect inmates from state authorities. The pastor's stepping in front of the police official to abet Lucas's evasion of arrest provides a vivid illustration of the complex intermediary space they occupy in prison. This pastor, Pastor Cicero, and Pastor Marcos all fit this paradigm of the Progressive Pentecostal response to potentially violent situations. In all of these instances pastors entered spaces of intense conflict or crises to protect an individual inmate or group of inmates whose lives were in immediate danger.

The second theme was that pastors' presence in these volatile spaces placed them in a moral and legal gray area. Lucas didn't order anything at the second café, so nobody gave him any financial support, either directly or indirectly.[3] But the intimacy of the relationships between pastors and prisoners like Lucas—as well as narco-gangs like the Comando Vermelho—is a double-edged sword. On one hand, pastors can use their respected position to quell violence or diffuse potentially violent situations. On the other, this space at the edge of the map of morality can be used to undermine a legitimate exercise of state authority or simply for personal gain. Pastors' relationships with gang-affiliated inmates could easily become a means to launder money, smuggle contraband, or relay valuable information to and from criminal leaders.

Stories of "corrupt" Pentecostal pastors swirled around Rio de Janeiro during the year I spent collecting data. A pastor who had been visiting the prisons in Rio for the past ten years told me about an offer made to him by the uncle of an infamous drug trafficker who was locked up at one of the maximum-security prisons in Rio. The man introduced himself to the pastor outside the prison and after thanking the pastor for the work he had been doing with his nephew and other inmates, the man offered to "bless" the pastor's ministry.

The "blessing" was a bit more complicated than dropping an envelope into the offering plate. Instead, the uncle offered to open a bank account that would be in the church's name but accessible by the uncle. He said that at the beginning of each month he would deposit a substantial sum, around 100,000 Reais (approximately US$30,000) into the account. Using the 10 percent tithing guideline favored in Pentecostal churches, the uncle would withdraw 90 percent of the money at the end of the month and the remaining 10 percent would stay as the "blessing," which the pastor could use as he saw fit.

When I visited this pastor's church, it was apparent that his buying into such a scheme would have dramatically improved his church's financial situation. His humble Assemblies of God church was just an extension of his house and frankly it needed a lot of work. The pastor confessed that he was momentarily tempted by the offer and started to rationalize the righteousness of accepting it, but he then declined in the most delicate terms. The gang leader's uncle did not press the issue any further, but added that he had made this offer to a number of other pastors in the city, and very few of them had refused it.

This incident is an example of how, in addition to its stabilizing effect, the regular physical presence of the pastors in prison can also open a door to illicit activity. Once again, I did not witness or have any direct knowledge of such schemes in the prisons and jails I visited, but I would be very surprised if this kind of wrongdoing had never happened among Pentecostals working in Rio's prisons. The "politics of presence" strategy depends heavily on the charisma of the pastor, and some charismatic individuals are easily corrupted by opportunities to acquire wealth and power.

Pastor Marcos Pereira provides another example of how pastors standing too close to the fire can get burned or can burn others. He has not mediated in any prison riots recently because he just finished serving time as an inmate himself. The pastor was arrested on May 7, 2013, on charges that he raped female members of his congregation. Beyond the rape charges, he was being investigated on charges of laundering drug money and even homicide.

Specifically, he was accused of having an illegal, clandestine relationship with the Comando Vermelho and of attempting to arrange the murder of a church member who threatened to go public with information that would prove the relationship existed. During my fieldwork rumors floated through the city that Pastor Marcos had agreements with imprisoned gang leaders. The material wealth he flaunted—a fleet of vintage cars, Rolex watches, and imported electronics—raised suspicions (mine included). But when high-ranking, fugitive drug traffickers were found hiding in his drug rehabilitation center outside the city, the police started to investigate those rumors more closely.

Pastor Marcos Pereira was recently released on habeas corpus after serving eighteen months in jail, and he is back at the LDAG church located on the outskirts of Rio. His imprisonment and highly publicized trial had a tremendous impact on how the public views pastors' presence inside Rio's prisons. I cannot comment on the innocence or guilt of Pastor Marcos, but his case nonetheless highlights the Achilles' heel of charismatic authority. The same charisma that offers pastors a privileged position inside prison can provide opportunities to engage in illicit activity for personal profit. The suspicion that Pentecostals have ulterior motives for working with inmates often hinders their ability to enlist non-Pentecostal allies around the issue of prison reform.

HOW TO SAVE LOST SHEEP?

In Pentecostal theology, the "one"—the individual—is at the center of the story. The spiritual, emotional, physical, and material well-being of the individual is the desire of the Creator of the Universe, as expressed in the words attributed to Jesus in the Bible. Biblical passages, such as the parable that Jesus tells in the fifteenth chapter of the Gospel of Luke, inform how Pentecostals approach their work in prisons:

> Now all the tax collectors and sinners were coming near to listen to him. And the Pharisees and the scribes were grumbling and saying, "This fellow welcomes sinners and eats with them."
>
> So he told them this parable: "Which one of you, having a hundred sheep and losing one of them, does not leave the ninety-nine in the wilderness and go after the one that is lost until he finds it? When he has found it, he lays it on his shoulders and rejoices. And when he comes home, he calls together his friends and neighbors, saying to them, 'Rejoice with me, for I have found my sheep that was lost.' Just so, I tell you, there will be more joy in heaven over one sinner who repents than over ninety-nine righteous persons who need no repentance."

Jesus is the shepherd in this allegory, and the lost sheep could be anyone who has not submitted their life to God. This teaching and many other teachings rooted in the New Testament emphasize the importance of individual salvation and have inspired Christians for centuries to go to tremendous effort to convince others to make a commitment to God as understood in orthodox Christianity.

The two sentences introducing the parable do more than set the scene for the telling of the story—they also shape Pentecostal action in prison. They show that Jesus sought out and embraced the people on the margins of society, the tax collectors, and the sinners. He shared meals with people that the established religious leaders of the day found despicable, even "killable." Rio's incarcerated population—along with the economically and socially marginalized dwellers of the *favelas* from which most of the inmates come—are arguably the modern-day Brazilian equivalent of those Bronze Age untouchables. In the Pentecostals' worldview, Jesus' life is the model for Christians to follow, and because Jesus engaged and affirmed the dignity of the marginalized outcast in his society, they should undertake that kind of engagement as well.

I include this biblical passage because it helps to understand the background narrative in the development of Pentecostal pastors' and volunteers' outreach toward Rio's prisons. First it declares that even if the people marked as "sinners" or tax collectors (one of the most stigmatized professions in the social context from which the New Testament emerged) have little or no worth in the social hierarchy, their individual lives are nonetheless precious to God. This belief motivates many pastors to expend great amounts of time and other resources to work with incarcerated individuals—they believe they are following Jesus' lead.

The passage also sheds light on why most Pentecostals do not directly engage in traditional political action or form institutionalized social movements. Each individual sheep is important, and when one strays from the flock toward the potential for danger, the shepherd drops everything to save it. The shepherd in this parable does not focus his efforts on reforming shepherding practices to decrease the likelihood of a sheep's going astray. This parable and others like it hold a lot of weight for a group that professes the desire to mirror the behaviors and virtues they perceive in the biblical account of the life of Jesus. For a socially engaged charismatic movement that takes passages like Luke 15 seriously, saving souls and rescuing lost sheep are the ardent Christian's primary occupations.

There are other reasons that the pastors and volunteers I observed and interviewed tended to focus their efforts on individual inmates or single prisons. Everywhere but inside of prison, Brazilian Pentecostalism is highly fragmented. I saw the effects of this diffuse and often chaotic organizational structure among many of the church groups that visited Rio's prisons. Each pastor led his or her own group of parishioners or volunteers into the prisons with no thought of partnering with other Pentecostal groups around common goals. The individual pastors used their charisma to open the prison doors, then pursued whatever "lost sheep" they felt they should save. There was not any sort of denominational body or overarching ministry guiding the direction of the disparate Pentecostal groups.

In fact, I rarely saw pastors from different churches working together in any meaningful way inside the prison. The radically decentered structure of Brazilian Pentecostalism is not conducive to the formation of voting blocks around contentious social issues like prison conditions. Moreover, Pentecostal pastors are generally more comfortable leading than following, which makes for an organizational kitchen with too many chefs and too few line cooks.

One of the drawbacks of the type of charisma that most Pentecostal pastors used to gain entrée to the prisons was that charismatic leaders often do not work well with others. Maybe a "Pentecostal Pope" would be useful directing the hundreds of volunteers working in the prisons? But that sort of top-down model would cut directly against the grain of Pentecostalism.

The charisma displayed by Pastors Marcos and Cicero was essential in their efforts to quell the Pedrinhas prison riot and intervene on behalf of Marcelo. These situations played to the pastors' strength as charismatic leaders and fit squarely in the center of the theology that animated their movement. The grinding long-term work necessary to bring about prison reform or structural change requires a willingness to compromise and forge partnerships that many charismatic Pentecostal pastors simply do not have. For reasons both theological and practical, most Brazilian Pentecostals have been unwilling to participate in this sort of coalitional work, especially while there are "lost sheep" needing to be saved.

Despite the professed reluctance of charisma-based Pentecostal movements to engage ongoing efforts to bring about prison reform or effect deep structural change in Rio's civic culture, I believe that the work of Antonio Costa illustrates the potential for the emergence of a form of "connected charisma." Pastor Antonio used his charismatic appeal to win the trust and respect of the inmates incarcerated in Salgado, but he also was able to work simultaneously with government officials and the media.

Pastor Antonio was a Presbyterian, not a Pentecostal. He didn't speak in tongues, never tried to exorcise a demon from anyone. In fact, he expressed deep reservations about some of the practices of the other pastors who visited Salgado. But the denominational differences meant very little to the prisoners themselves. They called him pastor and treated him with the same reverence that they showed toward Pastors Marcos and Cicero. The difference was that Pastor Antonio entered the prisons with a set of social connections that allowed him to make demands of the prison administration that the other pastors didn't have the leverage or the clout to make. As Pentecostalism makes further inroads into the Brazilian middle class, this sort of "connected charisma" can potentially serve as a means for Pentecostals to effect real change in how Rio's prisons are operated.

Finally, when some social activists—and even some social scientists— criticize Pentecostal pastors for not working on prison reform or other structural issues, they are essentially saying, "Why don't these pastors approach the situation like I would?"

One answer is that they are pastors, not activists or social scientists. Some of them participate in activist work, but their primary objective is to lead their churches and support the spiritual and physical welfare of their congregations. This is not to say that Pentecostal pastors are not able to participate in or even lead coalitional social justice movements. But that knack for coalition building is a key component in a different kind of skill set—and it's just not a skill that many Pentecostals have or care to develop.

The pastors I interviewed and observed placed little confidence in any political candidates, legislative initiatives, or promises of top-down prison reform. In fact many of them operated in parts of the city where the state had a very limited presence. With the exception of Pastor Antonio, none of the pastors I met made direct requests to state officials to improve the dreadful conditions in the prisons, to curb illegal detentions, or to stop prisoner abuse by the guards. Yet despite this apparent lack of political participation by the Pentecostals, I would argue that the pastors and volunteers who visit the prisons are engaged in a form of political action—a politics of presence—that has observable effects on institutions that most of them profess to have no interest in changing.

This argument grows out of my own observations and experiences inside Rio's prisons and in the *favelas*—as well as on the famed beaches—that constitute the Rio of today. When I first entered the cellblocks with the Pentecostal pastors, I was struck by, and privately critical of, their lack of outrage about the inhumane conditions. There were seventy to eighty men crammed into cells with only fifteen beds in unbearable heat.[4] Some inmates had been detained for nearly a year without formal charges, and others had died from wounds incurred during arrest that could have easily been treated.

I thought the pastors were turning a blind eye to the gross human rights violations and focusing simply on the spiritual realm. I was critical in part because I thought they were overlooking the political processes and social structures behind the human rights disaster that was growing in Rio's prisons. In other words, I was critical because they were not looking at the situation as a social scientist would. And they did not seem particularly excited about the social scientist's preferred remedy for social ills—traditional, coalition-focused political action.

But as I continued to visit the prisons, my initial judgments started to soften. One of the reasons my perceptions changed was that as I became more familiar with the city's jails and prisons through regular visits over many months, I also got used to the brutal environment—specifically, I became less appalled by the overcrowded cells, intense heat, and rampant corruption. After a few weeks, I expected my shirt to become heavy with sweat, and I was not shocked when I had to step over an obviously ill or wounded inmate lying unattended on the concrete floor. If someone had observed me in the cellblocks after I had become accustomed to the conditions, they might think that I, too, was blind to the corrupt social and institutional structures at the root of this injustice.

The criticisms I was so quick to make during the first week of fieldwork were no longer so clear-cut after my personal experience. I realized that pastors who had been visiting the jails for five or ten years may have gone through a similar process of acclimation. Also, for the pastors who led poor congregations in neighborhoods that were miles away from the glamorous beaches of Copacabana and Ipanema, the failure of the penal institution was not so shocking. It was just another aspect of the deep failure of the state to govern responsibly—and responsively—in their economically marginalized communities.

In Rio's poorest neighborhoods, the health, education, sanitation, and security conditions are abysmal, and they have been so for decades. Instead of "missing" or purposefully ignoring the institutional failures and structural inequalities that produce Rio's deplorable prisons, as I initially suspected, most of the pastors lived each day in the midst of these injustices and were intimately familiar with them. They may not have tweeted about what they knew or posted articles about prison reform on social media, but they understood the structural sources of injustice of their city much more thoroughly than I did.

Even though pastors rarely employed social movement rhetoric or strategies from political organizing to shape their prison ministries, their work achieved some of the same goals that progressive secular political activists might pursue. For example, the pastors were each at the head of an independent religious group that, taken together with other like-minded but independent Pentecostal groups, created a diffuse but nonetheless powerful solidarity movement with the city's most ostracized social group—prisoners. During the sermons in the cells, the Pentecostal pastors rarely framed the prisoners as victims of an unjust society that disproportionately punishes the poor and exonerates the socially connected for a fee. But neither did they subscribe to the dominant narrative in Rio that framed criminals as the source of the city's social problems and tolerated the horrid prison conditions and violent tactics employed by the police.

When the pastors embraced rapists, prayed with murderers, sang worship songs with drug dealers, and treated all of the inmates as people endowed with inherent worth, they were participating in an activity that subverted the social order. They signaled their solidarity with the most stigmatized population in Rio de Janeiro by calling them *irmão* (brother) instead of *bandido* (bandit) or *vagabundo* (bum). One pastor responded to the inmates' words of gratitude for his visit by saying, "I know that if I am ever in here in the future, you would come to visit me."

In short, the Pentecostals did not treat the inmates as if they were "killable."

The pastors also delivered this same countercultural message to unincarcerated citizens of Rio de Janeiro, principally the people in their own congregations. They recounted the successes and challenges of their week's work and asked members of the congregation to pray for the inmates in the prisons that the pastors visited. They also invited congregants to visit the prisons themselves and to get involved in the lives of the struggling families of the inmates.

These messages were often delivered in the neighborhoods that suffered the most from Rio de Janeiro's rampant criminal violence. Even though their testimonials were delivered inside a church and often in the context of a sermon, the pastors achieved the first thing that many political activists try to do: They raised a group's awareness about a particular social issue.

I saw the fruits of this messaging on a small scale when I visited the churches of the pastors who ministered in the prisons—there were ex-inmates in the pews. This is traditional social movement activity, but since it happens inside the walls of Pentecostal churches and is often framed in religious language, it is rarely recognized as a mechanism of positive social change.

Pentecostal pastors have used this politics of presence to persuade prison wardens to stop the murder of an inmate, negotiate truces during prison riots, and help reduce overcrowding in jails. Though some pastors become criminals themselves, and most operate without a sophisticated prison reform strategy, their presence inside Rio's prisons and jails has real effects on the political actors and institutions that enable the corruption in Rio's prison system. They are reformers of the larger system that they engage through the city's prisons, though the reforms they effect are largely unintentional.

CONCLUSION

FINAL QUESTIONS: SOME WITH ANSWERS, OTHERS WITHOUT

Marcio's mother died when he was ten years old. Her death altered the nature of his childhood and redirected the trajectory of his young life. "She was everything to us," he said, "she was always at home, the foundation of our family." Marcio's father worked long hours to provide for his wife and fifteen children, while his mother stayed at home and kept the family moving forward. She not only cleaned, clothed, and fed her children, but she also steered them away from the *boca de fumo* and the Comando Vermelho members who controlled their *favela*. When Marcio's mother died, everything fell apart.

With his mother gone and his dad away working, Marcio's curiosity went unchecked and he started to explore the side of the neighborhood that was once forbidden to him. He stopped going to school and made friends with boys in similar situations. Like moths to the flame, Marcio and his friends gravitated toward the periphery of the *boca de fumo*, where they admired the CV members and their guns, money, girls, and power. When Marcio started drinking and smoking at age thirteen, it was the young men of CV that he emulated. At fifteen he was an active Comando Vermelho member. The gang wasn't Marcio's only option, but the CV didn't have much competition.

Marcio's life took an unfortunate but predictable turn when he was sent to prison just after his eighteenth birthday. "That was a cruel and terrible place," Marcio said. "I was just eighteen years old, but I was thrown in with people who were serious criminals. I was scared, but I adapted and grew up in there." He arrived in prison scared, but not surprised. Marcio was one of many darker-skinned young men from his neighborhood who were locked up inside the prison. His gang affiliation transferred seamlessly from the street into the cellblocks and he spent three years obeying the familiar laws of the Comando Vermelho. But also like many young prisoners in Rio de Janeiro, Marcio heard the Pentecostal message from his fellow inmates and converted a few months before the end of his sentence. At twenty-two, he was released back into the world armed with a fledgling faith and good intentions.

DO THEY *REALLY* MEAN IT?

"My first release from prison?" Marcio reminisced. "Ah, it felt great. Freedom, you feel like you can do whatever you want, when you want. But I had people in my neighborhood waiting for me. They offered me an opportunity back into the life I was used to, and the crime." His good intentions and fresh Pentecostal identity didn't inoculate him against the familiar patterns and pleasures of his old neighborhood. Marcio had little formal education and no work experience. He was a known member of one of the most violent gangs in the world and had just got out of prison; prospective employers did not line up to interview him. Weeks after his release, Marcio had an assault rifle slung over his shoulder and was once again working for the gang. After three years in prison and a Pentecostal conversion, it was as if nothing had changed.

WAS MARCIO'S PRISON CONVERSION GENUINE?

At this point in his life, Marcio's jailhouse conversion didn't seem to have much impact on his life, which begs a question that could be asked of all incarcerated Pentecostals: Do they *really* mean it?

My short but sincere response is that answering that question is above my pay grade. No matter how robust the methodology, I contend that social scientists are not equipped to make judgments about the authenticity of anyone's religious commitments. Throughout the project, I never tried to determine whether the inmates in the prison churches "really" believed the theological premises of Pentecostalism. I did not think it was my place to do so. I did not push the men I interviewed to say more about their *beliefs* and I did not test the soundness or depth of their theology. Instead, I focused my questions, observations, and analysis on the inmates' religious practice and how the men lived their lives inside of prison. My work was a study of lived religion.

The inmates in Cinza and Salgado did not share my aversion to judging the sincerity of other people's religious commitments. The question of authenticity was front and center in prison subculture, and prisoners constantly evaluated each other's religious lives. Prison church leaders were concerned with the question of authenticity because their ability to exist was contingent on other prisoners viewing their collective faith practice as genuine. As long as the Pentecostals were known as a group who practiced what they preached, they would be protected from prison violence and allowed to occupy space in the prison.

The gang also had an interest in ensuring that the Prison Pentecostals were not just "hiding behind a Bible." In many cases, gang leaders permitted members to disavow their gang commitments in order to join the Pentecostals. If the gang members-turned-Pentecostals were deemed by the prison population to be insincere in their postgang religious practice, it would make the gang look like they were being taken advantage of and easily manipulated. Both groups dealt harshly with men whom they believed were just playing Pentecostal, but neither group relied on mere expressions of belief as the criteria for judgment. Gang members and prison church members observed the daily lives of the men in prison in order to gauge the sincerity of their faith commitments.

At first glance, studying religion inside of prison may seem like an exceptional research context because of the totalitarian hold that official and unofficial sources of authority exert over the lives of imprisoned men and women. In prison, ulterior motives are dramatically apparent and can cast a shadow of doubt on a person's faith. Still, in Rio's prisons, claiming to be a Pentecostal can decrease an inmate's vulnerability to violent attacks, potentially influence a judge's decision, or simply bolster a claim of personal reformation.

Even though these seem like strong forces, I am not convinced studying religion in prison is so different than studying religion in other
contexts. Name a place and a religion and I am certain there are factors beyond the "purely spiritual" that influence in some way an individual's affiliation and participation. People might go to their temple
in Bangalore, synagogue in Paris, mosque in Minneapolis, or church in
Lagos for spiritual fulfillment—and to look for spouses, curry parental
approval, deepen the groove of habit, search for entertainment, and so
on. That doesn't mean that a person is *only* attending because of those
reasons, but there are many factors operating simultaneously that all
might influence religious affiliation along with belief. Even though the
ulterior motivations seemed extraordinary, I did not feel the need to
pursue the question of authenticity from the belief perspective because
the situation in prison may not be any more or less complex than any
other context.

DOES IT WORK?

If appraising the authenticity of an inmate's faith requires the social
scientist to draw conclusions that are impossible to support with data,
what about using less subjective, quantifiable data like recidivism rates
to support conclusions based on behavior rather than belief? Most of
the men I met were still incarcerated when I left Brazil, so it is hard for
me to make any claims about the relationship between religious practice in prison and criminal behavior after prisoners' release. I am not
aware of any longitudinal studies on Brazilian, inmate-led churches
like Heroes for Christ to draw upon, but sociologists and criminol-
ogists have conducted extensive work in other settings on religion's
impact on inmates' desistance from crime once they are released from
prison. In fact, the question driving most social science research on
religion inside of prison is, "Does religion reduce recidivism?"

Byron Johnson (2011) published the most comprehensive work on
the subject by compiling and analyzing data from 273 social scientific
studies of faith-based programs inside of prison in the United States

and a handful of other countries, including Brazil, from 1944 to 2010. Johnson focused on studies that tracked inmates who participated in faith-based programming inside of prison and then followed them after their release. His aggregated analysis found that 90 percent of the studies reported decreased criminal activity postrelease, 8 percent reported no change in behavior, and 2 percent reported an increase in criminal behavior. Johnson summed up the basics of his argument in the title of his book—*More God, Less Crime*—which is a play on a phrase used by the pro-gun lobby: "more guns, less crime."

My guess based on this analysis is that if I followed the men in the prison churches in Cinza and Salgado as they finished their sentences and were released back to society, they would have considerably lower recidivism rates than the general population, especially the gang-affiliated inmates. My belief that the Pentecostal inmates would be less likely to commit crimes hinges on their continued Pentecostal practice outside of prison (which is not guaranteed), because those practices and the communities that cultivate them offer some very practical tools for former inmates who are trying to hold on at the sharp edges of society.

First, Pentecostalism's teetotaling requirements would reduce criminal behavior that is fueled by drugs and alcohol. In the United States alcohol is a factor in 40 percent of all violent crime, and in many of the interviews I conducted the sequence of events that led an individual to prison started with "I was drinking with friends at a bar."

Further, Pentecostalism's emphasis on men's participation in the domestic sphere encourages them to spend time with their families and not on the streets where trouble lurks. Ex-inmates do not fare well in the job market, and while very few churches hire people coming out of prison, Pentecostal participation can open new social networks that may lead to employment. Finally, Pentecostalism's demand on a person's time may seem like a burden, but it can actually be a useful asset in the months immediately following release. *Crentes* go to three, four, or five worship services a week, so there is less time to slide back into criminal behaviors.[1]

On the back cover of *More God, Less Crime*, the sociologist of religion Rodney Stark stated his approval of the book's conclusion with the ringing endorsement "Religion works!" To Stark and many proponents of faith-based prison programming, the proof that religion "works" lies in peer-reviewed studies that show a dramatic decrease in recidivism among inmates who participate in these programs compared to inmates who do not. There are always methodological questions with these sorts of studies, especially with sampling, but by looking at recidivism data alone, it is clear that these programs make a difference.

Before I started the fieldwork for the project, I felt I would need to directly address the question of whether or not religion in prison "works." Specifically, I wanted to be able to make a claim about prison religion's impact on larger society. Tracking religiously affiliated inmates who were not committing crimes once they were released from prison seemed like the best way to do that. Once I started the fieldwork, I abandoned this line of inquiry, but as I was writing this chapter, I looked through my original funding proposal and read the following line: "An inmate's conversion can only be proved genuine once he is released from prison." What I meant was that if an inmate leaves prison after a conversion and continues to participate in the same criminal activity that he pursued before his conversion, then the conversion must not have been genuine. Also implied was that if the inmate did not get arrested postconversion, "religion works" and the conversion must have been genuine. When I wrote the proposal, I thought I would advance the "works/doesn't work" model.

Linking religion and desistance from crime was appealing because it did not require me to make any judgments about the authenticity of an individual's religious practice, something I was determined not to do. Plus, recidivism rates felt objective. But when I looked back and saw what I wrote, I winced because that short sentence was saturated with theological implications that I did not intend to make. If I had implemented such an assumption into the research, I would have trivialized the religious lives of inmates by implying that their religious practice in prison was something less than what people outside of prison were practicing.

Thus one of my goals for this book is to detach studying prison religion from a concern for the relationship between religiosity and postrelease recidivism rates. I contend that the religious lives of inmates are worth studying apart from any impact they may have on future crime. Studying recidivism and highlighting ways to reduce rates are certainly worthy research pursuits, but studying inmates' lives is worthwhile beyond an examination of whether they commit more or fewer crimes. In fact, I would argue that the incarcerated Pentecostals' experience illuminates some of the reasons why the faith has been spread so widely since the Azusa Street Revival just over one hundred years ago.

ADAPTING AND EMPOWERING

Shortly after his release, Marcio returned to gang life and was up to his ears in his *favela*'s drug traffic. At that time in his life, it appeared as if his jailhouse conversion had made no impact on his criminal behavior. His Prison Pentecostal experience looked like an inconsequential phase that he went through as a young, scared inmate in Rio's most notorious prison. But Marcio was just twenty-two when he was released from prison for the first time, and it would have been too early in his history to reach that conclusion.

One evening, nine months after his first release from prison, Marcio was patrolling his neighborhood with a fellow CV member. Like moths to a different flame, the two gang members walked toward the Pentecostal hymns coming from a sound system set up in the street for a revival just a few hundred yards from the *boca de fumo* they protected. "We walked over to the edge of the crowd, and a friend of mine emerged and gave me a prophetic word," Marcio said. The friend knew Marcio's history, and the weapon he carried left no doubt about his current involvement with the CV. But in a move that reflects the relationship I observed between the gang and the Pentecostals in Rio de Janeiro, Marcio's friend was not intimidated or put off by his involvement with drugs and organized crime. In fact, his Pentecostal friend reached out and touched him. "He put his hand on my shoulder and prayed for me," Marcio said. "He told me, 'In five days, your life, your entire story will change.' "

At the time, Marcio was not sure what to make of his friend's proclamation. "I had my assault rifle hanging from my arm and I was high," Marcio said. "I smoked so much marijuana then, so I didn't really understand what he was saying. I thought 'What is he talking about?' I really didn't believe it. That was October 1st and two days later I was back in prison."

Marcio was arrested for a serious felony and spent October 3 and 4 in jail, which were the third and fourth days after his encounter with his friend at the street service. The jail was located very close to Marcio's neighborhood, and the police worried that the gang might mount an assault on the facility to break Marcio from the jail, so he was quickly transferred into Rio's maximum-security facility. Marcio was back in Bangu.

"When I arrived in Bangu it had been five days [since the Pentecostal street service]." The timing struck Marcio as more than a mere coincidence—he felt it was God trying to get his attention. Marcio recommitted his life to God on the concrete floor of his cellblock in Bangu, in front of the other inmates. It was his second profession of religious commitment inside of Bangu. "I got down on my knees and asked God for refuge. I cried for help and mercy and asked God to change my situation. I couldn't handle it anymore."

Marcio said that his second submission to God inside of prison was *verdadeiro* (true), and since it was done in front of the other inmates, he earned an invitation into the Pentecostal cellblock. "When I accepted Jesus, a guy came from the brothers' cells and told me, 'God is working in your life, this [the CV cells] is no longer your destiny.' So I moved to the brothers' cellblock, started to go to service every day, and began the work God had for me."

Marcio's move into the brothers' cellblock was more of a transfer than a departure from the prison's gang system. He left the Comando Vermelho and joined a gang of Pentecostals.

Prison church members were reluctant to compare their groups to a gang during the interviews. In their minds, gangs and churches don't mix. But as I explained earlier in the book, the organizational similarities and other ganglike characteristics of the prison churches were crucial for their survival inside of prison. If the prison churches were carbon copies of Pentecostal churches on the outside, or operated by official prison ministries, I doubt they would have been able to withstand the pressures inside the cellblocks.

But a ganglike organizational structure only partly explains the churches' success. Prison Pentecostalism depends on charismatic leaders, but, given the location, the pool of potential leaders is limited. Still, prison churches grow into independent, self-sustaining groups because pastors, deacons, and worship leaders arise from within the inmate population and lead. Prison Pentecostalism would not be an institutionalized presence throughout Rio's criminal justice system if it were not able to empower indigenous leadership. The incarcerated leader preaches, sings, prays, fasts, suffers, and praises alongside the other church members. Inmates not only set the vision for the future of the prison churches, they also negotiate with gang and prison officials and make themselves available to meet the spiritual and sometimes physical and emotional needs of inmates twenty-four hours a day.

In prison, Marcio's fellow church members served as his mentors, friends, protectors, and brothers in Christ. He lived life together with these men. They ate meals together, worshipped together, shared family visiting time with each other, and shared the common pain associated with incarcerated life. I was able to observe the power of this shared suffering most clearly during the worship songs as men wept openly and consoled other men who were having an especially difficult day. Their shared tribulation created a bond between the church members (and likely the gang members as well) akin to the types of friendships that some soldiers form with each other on the battlefield.

Prison Pentecostalism's theology was certainly flavored by the prison context, but it did not stray far from the beliefs and practices of mainstream Brazilian Pentecostalism. The prison groups held on to the basic tenets of the faith even though their churches at times looked like prison gangs and were led by convicted criminals. Their orthodox theology and practice kept them connected to the larger body of churches in Brazil and provided an identity, not always recognized by everyone, that was more than just being a criminal.

After four years in the brothers' cells, Marcio left Bangu for the second time. His second experience as an incarcerated Pentecostal was more intense than his first. His four years living in the brothers' cells turned out to be like four years in a monastery. When he was released for a second time, Marcio was almost five years older than he had been at the time of his first release. But he still faced a difficult transition because he had never been formally employed; his rap sheet had more lines than his resume and his record with reentry attempts was 0 for 1. When people in his old neighborhood saw Marcio on the streets dressed as a Pentecostal, they were skeptical that his second release would lead to different results than his first. "My friends didn't believe it," Marcio said. "They had to see it with their own eyes. They invited me to smoke with them, go to prostitutes, deal drugs, and be a murderer again." Those were the same invitations he had received and accepted after his first release, but Marcio said his mindset was different this time. He knew the stakes were high and that he was fortunate even to have a chance at making a life for himself outside of prison.

"For me it was a privilege," Marcio said about his second release, "because many people die inside of prison; they don't get another chance." To Marcio, taking advantage of that opportunity meant maintaining his faith. "When a believer leaves prison, he has to cement his commitment to God and reconstruct everything he lost." He took a step to cement his commitment to God by joining a small church in the middle of a dilapidated shantytown less than a mile from where he was born.

A NEW LIFE

Igreja Evangélical Pentecostal Ebenezer (Pentecostal Evangelical Church Ebenezer) was a small, independent Pentecostal church located on the banks of a putrid stream on an unpaved path deep in the middle of a neighborhood dominated by the Comando Vermelho. It was (and still is) a humble church outfitted with basic ceramic tile on the floor, white plastic chairs, and handwritten signs and posters pinned to the walls. The church has never had to worry about parking because all of its members walk from their homes or the nearest bus station. There have been few car owners in the history of the church.

When Marcio arrived after his release from prison, he also arrived on foot. He may have been an intimidating figure when he walked through the door, but he said the congregation embraced him, as did the pastor. Pastor Hélio, the church's leader, took a particular interest in Marcio's life. He knew Marcio's story and offered to help guide Marcio through the transition from prison to society. The touchstones of Pastor Hélio's plan were family, church, and work.

The pastor told Marcio it was time to become a man. He said Marcio ought to work, no matter how menial the task or small the pay, and he encouraged Marcio to marry his girlfriend. Marcio did both. Three years after Marcio's second release from prison, he was married, a construction worker, and an active church member. Pastor Hélio saw leadership potential in Marcio and approached him about becoming a deacon in the church. The pastor was very specific about what was required of Marcio if he were to assume a leadership position in the church: "You need to have a good testimony and be a good husband, a great father, and honor your family. You need to honor those who love you and those close to you."

Once again, the sincerity of Marcio's faith would be judged by the way he lived his daily life. If Pastor Hélio required a minimal level of educational attainment, a clean criminal record, or experience in the workplace, Marcio would have had little chance of rising to a position of authority in the church. He didn't insist Marcio speak in tongues or take the "right" stand on every theological issue; instead, he watched and evaluated how Marcio lived.

Seven years after Marcio first attended the church and three years after he became a deacon, Pastor Hélio was diagnosed with terminal cancer. Knowing he would soon die, he set the succession plan in motion. He didn't contact the headquarters of a denomination—Igreja

Evangélical Pentecostal Ebenezer was an independent church—nor did he reach out to local seminaries to look for a young, up-and-coming preacher. He didn't try to lure a pastor away from another, smaller church with the promise of a larger congregation. Pastor Hélio looked no further than his own congregation for the church's next pastor.

Twice incarcerated, a former gang member with a middle school education and a violent past, Marcio may have seemed an unlikely pastoral candidate. But this is one of the reasons Pentecostalism has spread so deeply into the marginalized segments of Brazilian society. Pentecostal churches have empowered socially stigmatized Brazilians and historically disenfranchised individuals. When Pastor Hélio evaluated Marcio, he saw a life that had been changed and the "good testimony" that Marcio had built over the seven years since his last day in prison—those key qualities qualified Marcio for the job.

SAVE THE SINNER OR SAVE THE SOCIETY?

Throughout Marcio's gang career Pentecostals reached out to "save" him. Until he went to prison, Marcio ignored all of them. He thought that Pentecostalism was "something from the past, something for cowards." Neighborhood Pentecostals worked tirelessly to save Marcio's soul, but their keen focus on Marcio's spiritual life raises questions about their concern for his earthly surroundings.

There is abundant evidence that Pentecostal leaders and laypeople are committed to improving the lives of Rio's poorest, sickest, most marginalized, and most stigmatized. There is considerably less evidence that they are concerned with improving the neighborhoods and societies where these people live. Marcio's rise from prisoner to pastor is inspirational and illuminates some of the ways that Pentecostal affiliation can contribute to an inmate's successful transition to society, but it is nonetheless a story saturated with pain and suffering. The death of his mother was an unavoidable tragedy, but he was born into one of the worst neighborhoods in one of the most violent cities in the world. It was also a city full of Pentecostals.

Did the Pentecostals in Marcio's neighborhood seek to change the structural inequalities that shaped Marcio's life from the day he was born? Did they try to improve the horrid education system in the neighborhood? Did they press local government agencies to clean the river next to Marcio's church that collected the raw sewage from hundreds of houses and smelled worse than month-old eggs? Did they push back against the blatant racism that neighborhood residents often faced? Did they march to the steps of City Hall to protest a murderous police force? Did they ever try to get the Comando Vermelho out of the neighborhood?

Finally, is Marcio's neighborhood, which is simultaneously filled with Pentecostal churches and shaped by structural oppression, a case in point for those who argue that religion simply numbs and distracts the masses as a way to ensure their ongoing oppression?

In chapter 6, I described how Pentecostals intervened in violent situations on behalf of vulnerable prisoners—a practice that I called a politics of presence. I argued that while Pentecostal volunteers visiting the prison were not apolitical actors, they did not necessarily employ a strategy that relied on traditional political tactics. Do the Pentecostals living, working, and worshipping in the *favelas* employ a politics of presence by being there, and, if so, does it make a difference?

None of these questions can be answered with a simple yes or no, but I have said that studying religion inside of prison can deepen our understanding of the relationship between religious belief and society, so they are fair questions to pose. One way to address these issues is to compare Pentecostal forms of social engagement with Protestant churches in another time and place. Compared to black churches in the American South during the civil rights movement, Brazilian Pentecostal churches have not come close to reaching their potential in changing unjust social structures.

Aldon Morris (1986) argued that the small, locally led black churches throughout the southeastern United States served as "local movement centers" to organize resistance to an oppressive regime. Morris thought scholars underestimated the role of these churches and undercut the importance of their agency to the movement: "Social Scientists for too long have portrayed the masses as a flock of sheep reacting blindly to uncontrollable forces" (vi).

Morris did not see the pastors and members of black churches in the US South as blind sheep; in fact, he identified the particular qualities of the black church that enabled it to be such an effective force of resistance against institutional racism in the Jim Crow South:

> In the case of the civil rights struggle, the preexisting black church provided the early movement with the social resources that made it a dynamic force, in particular leadership, institutionalized charisma, finances, an organized following, and an ideological framework through which passive attitudes were transformed into collective consciousness supportive of collective action. (77)

The Pentecostal churches in Rio display many of these same qualities. Using Morris's analysis, it is reasonable to conclude that the Pentecostal churches in neighborhoods like Marcio's, and even those inside the prisons and jails in Rio de Janeiro, share much in common with the black churches involved in the American civil rights movement of the 1950s and 1960s. Both groups empowered indigenous leaders and employed institutional charisma through the role of the pastor, and neither the black churches in the United States nor the Pentecostal church in Rio depend on financial assistance from the state or elite social classes. The glaring difference between the two groups is that unlike black churches in the South in the 1960s, Rio's Pentecostal groups have not leveraged their strengths and resources to create anything nearly as game-changing as the US civil rights movement. Rio's Pentecostal groups have yet to be able to transform passive attitudes on social injustice into "collective consciousness supportive of collective action."

The reasons for this difference are complex and debatable, but there are a few contextual distinctions that may help to explain the Pentecostal churches' seeming complacency. First, the social exclusion suffered by African Americans in the mid-twentieth century and the plight of the "killable people" in Rio de Janeiro are similar in important ways—most importantly, they are both groups with direct ties to slavery that have been historically oppressed. On the other hand, one of the differences between the two groups is that legalized segregation in the US South provided a visible, well-understood target toward which religious leaders could direct their efforts. Integrating lunch counters, buses, and public schools provided tangible goals around which to organize civil disobedience and protests. In twenty-first-century Brazil, social segregation is alive and well, but it is not enforced through legislative means and is thus woven into the Brazilian social fabric in a different way than it was in the United States. Legally, anyone can board a bus in Rio, sit on a public beach, or attend a public school, and every citizen is required to vote. Rio's social inequality is inarguably racialized, but it does not rely on a set of Jim Crow laws that might catalyze collective action for change.

Rio's *favelas* and the segregated neighborhoods of Montgomery, Atlanta; Mobile, Alabama; and Memphis, Tennessee, are useful comparisons, but only up to a point. The social and historical contexts of these places are profoundly different and one cannot expect that social change will or should occur in the same way.

DIGNITY

Because of these similarities and differences, I am simultaneously hopeful and skeptical that Brazilian Pentecostalism will bring about profound social change in Rio de Janeiro and throughout the country. But divining the future in that way is not at the heart of this book. Dignity is my central argument and I contend that dignity is the driving force behind Pentecostal practice inside of the prison and jails I studied.

The writings of Howard Thurman—the scholar, mystic, and pastor—have more than anything else shaped my understanding of the role of dignity in Prison Pentecostalism. Thurman wore many hats during his career. He founded and pastored the first intentionally multiracial church, Church for the Fellowship of All Peoples (Fellowship Church) in San Francisco, and served as the political and spiritual advisor to civil rights leaders, including Martin Luther King Jr., who carried a copy of Thurman's book *Jesus and the Disinherited* in his briefcase. But Thurman resisted pleas to play a more visible role in political and social movements. Even though he was profoundly influenced by the time he spent with Mahatma Gandhi in 1935, Thurman chose to counsel and inspire civil rights leaders instead of joining them on the picket lines.

Thurman delivered a series of lectures at Harvard Divinity School in 1947 on Negro spirituals sung by American slaves that were published in two books, *Deep River* (1945) and *The Negro Spiritual Speaks of Life and Death* (1947). In these lectures and books, Thurman focused on the religious practices of slaves. These components of Thurman's work constituted a "lived religion" project long before the term was used to describe a particular methodology.

Social scientists of the 1940s often pushed Thurman to adopt a more mainstream interpretation of the slaves' worship as a form of escapism and ultimately as a tool of oppression deployed by the white slaveholders. Thurman's idiosyncratic interpretation of slave spirituals was contested by a scholarly community that was largely white and secular. But some African Americans were also hesitant to embrace these songs with the reverence of the previous generation. Thurman responded to these critiques and reservations directly:

> Again and again I have heard many people (including descendants of these singers) speak disparagingly of the otherworldly emphasis as purely a mechanism of escape and sheer retreat. The argument is that such an emphasis served as a kind of soporific, making for docility and submission. (2003, 42)

Thurman countered that using Marx's opiate analogy to simply write off oppressed people's faith in the supernatural fails to recognize religion's ability to instill self-respect in the believer and enable him or her to persevere through dreadful circumstances. He encouraged his fellow African Americans in the 1940s and 1950s to be proud of a faith that gave the slaves a "strange new courage." In a response to the Marxist critique, Thurman concluded, "Religious emphasis did not paralyze action, it did not make for mere resignation. On the contrary, it gave the mind a new dimension of resourcefulness" (1998, 72).

Though more than a century after and a hemisphere away from the religious lives of the slaves that Thurman studied, I saw these same themes manifested in the lives of some of the Pentecostal inmates I encountered in Rio de Janeiro. There were moments when I witnessed Pentecostal hymns serve "to deepen the capacity of endurance and the absorption of suffering" for inmates inside of Salgado and Cinza and their captive faith provided the "raw material out of which they fashioned a hope that their environment in all of its cruelty, could not crush" (Thurman 1998, 71).

I also saw this endurance, hope, and dignity on display in the lives of ex-inmates. When Marcio reflected on his current position as the lead pastor of Igreja Evangélical Pentecostal Ebenezer, he told me, "I am happy because for an ex-trafficker, to be transformed and to have God put this sort of responsibility in my hands is a great honor." I saw him pray for, console, and inspire people in his neighborhood who were going through circumstances more difficult than any I could imagine enduring. I saw how neighborhood youth, especially young men, were drawn to him and the faith he had discovered inside Bangu's cellblocks. They wanted to be like him in the same way that Marcio had wanted to be like the Comando Vermelho members when he was a teenager.

Marcio's Pentecostalism and his position as pastor did not bring him wealth, political clout, or a ticket out of the *favela*. He lived less than a mile from where he was born, worked minimum-wage construction jobs during the day, and pastored the church at night and on the weekends. But his faith brought him dignity. He captured the heart of what I argue fuels the Prison Pentecostalism I studied when I asked him what his faith has brought to his life:

> Because of Jesus Christ, wherever I go, I am no longer known as Lil'
> Marcio the drug trafficker, the Comando Vermelho member. I am no
> longer seen as Lil' Marcio the murderer or Lil' Marcio the criminal. No,
> I am now seen as Marcio, a man. A man called to preach the gospel.
> I am seen as the father of a family, a guy who got married, who changed
> his life. I am now known as a pastor, a man of God.

With all of its seeming blindness to structural injustice, emphasis on unseen spiritual forces, and uncomfortable biblical literalism, Pentecostalism nonetheless provided inmates with a religious practice that enabled them to live moral and meaningful lives in the midst of intense hardship. It resisted the notion that they were killable and encouraged them to walk with their heads held high. Prison Pentecostalism provided Rio's inmates the raw material that "enabled them to reject annihilation and affirm a terrible right to live" (Thurman 1998, 71).

NOTES

INTRODUCTION

1. Candelária Church in downtown Rio was the site of the 1993 massacre where a vigilante group comprising in part off-duty police officers murdered eight children who were sleeping on the church steps.
2. The names of these two institutions are pseudonyms. I also used pseudonyms for all of the inmates I interviewed in an effort to protect their identity.
3. See http://www.economist.com/node/21563288.
4. The "Golden Law" was signed on May 13, 1888, and officially abolished slavery in Brazil.

CHAPTER 1

1. Salgado is a pseudonym for the jail's real name in order to protect the identity of the inmates and the jail's administration officials.
2. Since I conducted the fieldwork, the city of Rio de Janeiro reorganized the prison system and Salgado, and many jails like it have since closed.
3. See http://oglobo.globo.com/rio/masmorra-medieval-carceragem-da-polinter-registra-567-graus-3054340.
4. All of the inmates' names used in this book are pseudonyms.

CHAPTER 2

1. See http://www.riodepaz.org.br/blog/20/estatistica-oficial-de-mortes-violentas-desaparecidos-e-tentativas-de-homicidio.

2. See http://www.telegraph.co.uk/news/worldnews/southamerica/
brazil/8882701/Rio-favelas-key-facts-and-figures.html.

3. See https://medium.com/jornalistas-livres/os-defensores-do-
impeachment-s%C3%A3o-brancos-1d37d7da0698.

4. The armed guard in front of a *favela* is not an invention of the gang.
Many *favelas* began as land invasions—mostly by migrants from
the northeast. Once the land was occupied, the group of new dwellers would place one or two armed men at the entrance to ensure
that nobody would come to remove the soon-to-be neighborhood
(Goldstein 2003).

CHAPTER 3

1. See http://www.diariodovale.com.br/noticias/0,42647,%27Leandro-
da-Minerlandia%27-sera-julgado-terca-feira-em-Barra-Mansa.
html#axzz3aqgcl5RF.

2. See http://revistaepoca.globo.com/Epoca/0,6993,EPT735313-1664-
1,00.html.

3. See http://www.chesnuttarchive.org/classroom/lynching_table_
year.html.

4. Macumba is an Afro-Brazilian religion, which is a delicate mix of
African spirit worship with Roman Catholic imagery. Thought by
many Pentecostals to be satanic, it is often targeted as the front line
of spiritual warfare.

CHAPTER 4

1. One of the unusual manifestations of police corruption in Rio is the
illegal sale of police-issued firearms and uniforms on Rio's black
market. The utility of the guns is fairly obvious, but the uniforms
are also useful for criminal activities. The weapons and uniforms
both command prices that are many times the monthly salary of
a police officer and are sold, or rented, to the gangs by corrupt
police officers. See http://noticias.terra.com.br/brasil/noticias/0,,
OI1544031-EI5030,00-Criminoso+se+exibe+no+Orkut+com+farda
+da+policia.html and http://noticias.terra.com.br/brasil/noticias/0,,

OI1090147-EI316,00-Comando+Vermelho+invade+morro+e+mata
+dois+no+Rio.html.

2. See http://www.wiltonlima.com.br/2011/02/monstro-de-pinheiro-
e-decapitado-em.html.

CHAPTER 6

1. None of the inmates' real names are used in this chapter.

2. Danlio Fernandes, "De Missionário Nas Prisões à Pastor Sonic," *Genizah*, July 8, 2010.

3. In this situation, my role crossed into something besides an objective, uninvolved observer. It was not my intention to occupy this role when I began the research, but, given the position I found myself in, I tried to do what I thought was best.

4. Antônio Werneck, ' "Masmorra Medieval': Carceragem da Polinter Registra 56,7 Graus," *Globo*, February 11, 2010.

CONCLUSION

1. Some of the best work on Pentecostalism's impact on men living in the margins of cities in North, Central, and South America illustrates how these processes work for ex-inmates better than I can (Brenneman 2011; Flores 2013; Smilde 2007).

BIBLIOGRAPHY

Abbott, Andrew. 1997. "On the Concept of Turning Point." *Comparative Social Research* 16: 89–109.

Allen, Marshall. 2006, April 15. "Pentecostal Movement Celebrates Humble Roots L.A.'s Azusa Street to Mark Centennial of Fast-Growing Religion Centered on Holy Spirit." *Washington Post*, https://www.washingtonpost.com/archive/local/2006/04/15/pentecostal-movement-celebrates-humble-roots-span-classbankheadlas-azusa-street-to-mark-centennial-of-fast-growing-religion-centered-on-holy-spiritspan/99f69d68-e65e-44d4-87eb-6b192056d0e8/?utm_term=.506fe7dd3318.

Alves, M., and P. Evanson. 2011. *Living in the Crossfire: Favela Residents, Drug Dealers, and Police Violence in Rio de Janeiro.* Philadelphia: Temple University Press.

Anderson, Allan. 2006. "Revivals and the Global Expansion of Pentecostalism after Azusa Street." In *The Azusa Street Revival and Its Legacy*, edited by Cecil M. Robeck Jr. and Harold D. Hunter, 175–191. Cleveland, TN: Pathway Press.

Arias, Enrique. 2006. *Drugs and Democracy in Rio de Janeiro: Trafficking, Social Networks, and Public Security.* Chapel Hill: University of North Carolina Press.

Billingsley, Scott. 2008. *It's a New Day: Race and Gender in the Modern Charismatic Movement.* Tuscaloosa: University of Alabama Press.

Bomann, Rebecca Pearl. 1999. *Faith in the Barrios: The Pentecostal Poor in Bogota.* Boulder, CO: Lynne Rienner.

Brenneman, Robert. 2011. *Homies and Hermanos: God and Gangs in Central America.* New York: Oxford University Press.

Brusco, Elizabeth. 1995. *The Reformation of Machismo: Evangelical Conversion and Gender in Colombia.* Austin: University of Texas Press.

Burdick, John. 1993. "Struggling against the Devil: Pentecostalism and Social Movements in Urban Brazil." In *Rethinking Protestantism in Latin America*, edited by Virginia Garrard-Burnett and David Stoll, 20–44. Philadelphia: Temple University Press.

——. 1993. *Looking for God in Brazil*. Berkeley: University of California Press.

——. 1999. "What Is the Color of the Holy Spirit? Pentecostalism and Black Identity in Brazil." *Latin American Research Review* 34(2): 109–131.

——. 2005. "Why Is the Black Evangelical Movement Growing in Brazil?" *Journal of Latin American Studies* 37(2): 311–332.

Cadge, W., P. Levitt, and D. Smilde. 2011. "De-centering and Re-centering: Rethinking Concepts and Methods in the Sociological Study of Religion." *Journal for the Scientific Study of Religion* 50: 437–444.

Cano, Ignacio. 1997. *Letalidade da Ação Policial no Rio de Janeiro*. Rio de Janeiro: Instituto de Estudos da Religião.

Cano, Ignacio, and Eduardo Ribeiro. 2007. "Homicídios no Rio de Janeiro e no Brasil: Dados, Políticas Públicas e Perspectivas." In *Homicidios no Brasil*, edited by Marcus Vinicius Gonçalves da Cruz, 51–78. Rio de Janeiro: FGV Editora.

Cano, Ignacio, and Nilton Santos. 2007. *Violencia Letal, Renda e Desigualdade no Brasil*. Rio de Janeiro: 7 Letras.

Chesnut, R. Andrew. 1997. *Born Again in Brazil: The Pentecostal Boom and the Pathogens of Poverty*. New Brunswick, NJ: Rutgers University Press.

The Chesnutt Digital Archive. *Lynchings, by Year and Race, 1882–1968*. http://www.chesnuttarchive.org/classroom/lynching_table_year.html.

Clemmer, Donald. 1940. *The Prison Community*. Boston: Christopher Publishing House.

Cohen, Albert K. 1955. *Delinquent Boys: The Culture of the Gang*. Glencoe, IL: Free Press.

Cox, Harvey. 1995. *Fire from Heaven: The Rise of Pentecostal Spirituality and the Reshaping of Religion in the Twenty-First Century*. New York: Addison-Wesley.

Da Cunha, Euclides. 1944. *Rebellion in the Backlands (Os Sertoes)*. Chicago: University of Chicago Press.

Davenport, Keith. 2008. *Azusa Revisited*. New York: Lulu.

Davis, Mike. 1992. *City of Quartz: Excavating the Future in Los Angeles.* New York: Vintage.

———. 2006. *Planet of Slums.* New York: Verso.

The Economist. 2012, September 22.

Edgell, Penny. 2012. "A Cultural Sociology of Religion: New Directions." *Annual Review of Sociology* 38: 247–265.

Fausto, Boris. 1999. *A Concise History of Brazil.* Cambridge: Cambridge University Press.

Fernandes, Danilo. 2010, July 8. "A Seita do Pastor Marcos Pereira." *Genizah.*

Flores, Edward. 2013. *God's Gangs: Barrio Ministry, Masculinity, and Gang Recovery.* New York: NYU Press.

Fluker, Walter, and Catherine Tumber. 1998. *A Strange Freedom: The Best of Howard Thurman on Religious Experience and Public Life.* Boston: Beacon.

Frank, Zephyr. 2004. *Dutra's World: Wealth and Family in Nineteenth-Century Rio de Janeiro.* Albuquerque: University of New Mexico Press.

Freston, Paul. 1994. "Popular Protestants in Brazilian Politics: A Novel Turn in Sect-State Relations." *Social Compass* 41(4): 537–570.

Gabrielson R., R. Grochowski Jones, and E. Sagara. 2014, October 10. "Deadly Force, in Black and White." *ProPublica.*

Garcia-Navarro, Lulu. 2014, November 9. "In Brazil, Race Is a Matter of Life and Violent Death." *National Public Radio.*

Globo. 2014, July 21. "*Gravação em carro de polícia liga policiais a morte de menor no Rio.*" *Globo.com.* http://g1.globo.com/rio-de-janeiro/noticia/2014/07/video-incrimina-policiais-que-mataram-menor-no-sumare-no-rio.html.

Goffman, Erving. 1956. *The Presentation of Self in Everyday Life.* Edinburgh: University of Edinburgh Press.

———. 1961. *Asylums: Essays on the Social Situations of Mental Patients and Other Inmates.* Oxford: Doubleday.

Goldstein, Donna M. 2003. *Laughter Out of Place: Race, Class, Violence, and Sexuality in a Rio Shantytown.* Berkeley: University of California Press.

Guilherme, George. 2004, June 1. "Controversial Pastor Mediates End to Three-Day Prison Riot in Brazil: Minister Hopes Fame Will Allow Him Greater Access to Brazil's Prisons." *Christianity Today.* http://www.christianitytoday.com/ct/2004/juneweb-only/6-7-21.0.html.

Hallet, Michael, et al. 2015. ' "First Stop Dying': Angola's Christian Seminary as Positive Criminology." *International Journal of Offender Therapy and Comparative Criminology*, 1–19. Published online before print August 5, 2015, doi:10.1177/0306624X1559817.

Hunter, Harold D. 2006. "A Journey Toward Racial Reconciliation: Race Mixing in the Church of God of Prophecy." In *The Azusa Street Revival and Its Legacy*, edited by Cecil M. Robeck Jr. and Harold D. Hunter, 277–296. Cleveland, TN: Pathway Press.

Instituto de Seguranca Público. 2012, July 20. *Dados Oficiais*. http://www.isp.rj.gov.br/Conteudo.asp?ident=150.

Irwin, John, and Donald R. Cressey. 1962. "Thieves, Convicts and the Inmate Culture." *Social Problems* 10: 142–155.

Jacobs, James B. 1977. *Stateville: The Penitentiary in Mass Society*. Chicago: University of Chicago Press.

Jenkins, Philip. 2002. *The Next Christendom: The Coming of Global Christianity*. New York: Oxford University Press.

———. 2006. *The New Faces of Christianity: Believing the Bible in the Global South*. New York: Oxford University Press.

Johnson, Byron. 2011. *More God, Less Crime: Why Faith Matters and How It Could Matter More*. West Conshohocken, PA: Templeton.

Leeds, Elizabeth. 1996. "Cocaine and Parallel Polities in the Brazilian Urban Periphery: Constraints on Local-Level Democratization." *Latin American Research Review* 31: 47–83.

Madden, Lori. 1993. "The Canudos War in History." *Luso-Brazilian Review* 30(2), Special Issue: "The World Out of Which Canudos Came." (Winter 1993): 7.

Manza, Jeff, and Christopher Uggen. 2006. *Locked Out: Felon Disenfranchisement and American Democracy*. Oxford: Oxford University Press.

Mariz, C. L. 1994. *Coping with Poverty*. Philadelphia: Temple University Press.

Mariz, Cecilia L., and Maria d. D. C. Machado. 1998. "Recent Changes in the Scope of Brazilian Religion." *Social Compass* 45(3): 359–378.

Martin, David. 1990. *Tongues of Fire: The Explosion of Protestantism in Latin America*. Oxford: Basil Blackwell.

———. 1991. "The Economic Fruits of the Spirit." In *The Culture of Entrepreneurship*, edited by Bridgitte Berger, 73–84. San Francisco: Institute for Contemporary Studies.

———. 2002. *Pentecostalism: The World Their Parish*. Malden, MA: Blackwell.

Masci, David. 2014, November 14. "Why Has Pentecostalism Grown So Dramatically in Latin America?" Pew Research Center website.

Miller, Donald E., and Tetsunao Yamamori. 2007. *Global Pentecostalism: The New Face of Christian Social Engagement*. Berkeley: University of California Press.

Miranda, Ana Paula, and Maria Vitoria Pita. 2011. "Bureaucratic Regimes and State Languages: The Politics of Statistical Criminal Records on Violent Deaths in Rio de Janeiro and Buenos Aires." *Revista de Sociologia e Política*. SciELO Brasil.

Morris, Aldon. 1986. *The Origins of the Civil Rights Movement: Black Communities Organizing for Change*. Bloomington: Indiana University Press.

O Dia. 2009, November 20. "Identificado Suspeito de Expulsar Pastor em Favela do Rio." *O Dia Online*.

———. 2006, August 7. "Comando Vermelho Invade Morro e Mata dois no Rio." *O Dia Online*.

Ottoboni, Mario. 2003. *Transforming Criminals: An Introduction to the APAC Methodology*. Washington, DC: Prison Fellowship International.

Page, Joshua. 2011. *The "Toughest Beat": Politics, Punishment, and the Prison Officers' Union in California*. New York: Oxford University Press.

Penglase, Ben. 2005. "The Shutdown of Rio de Janeiro: The Poetics of Drug Trafficker Violence." *Anthropology Today* 21(5): 3–6.

———. 2014. *Living with Insecurity in a Brazilian Favela: Urban Violence and Daily Life*. New Brunswick, NJ: Rutgers University Press.

Pereira, Rafael. 2004, May 31. "Sob as leis do tráfico." *Epoca* (http://revistaepoca.globo.com/Epoca/0,6993,EPT735313-1664-2,00.html)

Perlman, Janet. 1976. *Myth of Marginality: Urban Poverty and Politics in Rio de Janeiro*. Berkeley: University of California Press.

———. 2010. *Favela: Four Decades of Living on the Edge in Rio de Janeiro*. New York: Oxford University Press.

Phillips, Tom. 2010, November 28. "Rio Reborn, Declares Mayor, as Police Recapture Infamous Drug Gang Slum." *Guardian*.

Piché, Justin, and Kevin Walby. 2010. "Problematizing Carceral Tours." *British Journal of Criminology* 50(3): 570–581.

Rolim, Francisco. 1995. *Pentecostalism. Brasil e America Latina*. Petropolis: Vozes.

Smilde, David. 2007. *Reason to Believe: Cultural Agency in Latin American Evangelicalism*. Berkeley: University of California Press.

Stoll, David. 1990. *Is Latin America Turning Protestant? The Politics of Evangelical Growth*. Berkeley: University of California Press.

Sykes, Gresham. 1958. *The Society of Captives*. Princeton, NJ: Princeton University Press.

Synan, Vinson. 2003. *Voices of Pentecost: Testimonies of Lives Touched by the Holy Spirit*. Ann Arbor, MI: Vine.

Tavory, Iddo, and Daniel Winchester. 2012. "Experiential Careers: The Routinization and De-routinaization of Religious Life." *Theory and Society* 41(4): 351–373.

Telegraph. 2011, November 10. "Rio Favelas: Key Facts and Figures."

Telles, Edward. 2004. *Race in Another America: The Significance of Skin Color in Brazil*. Princeton, NJ: Princeton University Press.

Thrasher, F. M. 1927. *The Gang*. Chicago: University of Chicago Press.

Thurman, Howard. 1947. *The Negro Spiritual Speaks of Life and Death, Being the Ingersoll Lecture on the Immortality of Man*. New York: Harper and Brothers.

———. 1998. *A Strange Freedom: The Best of Howard Thurman on Religious Experience and Public Life*, edited by Walter Earl Fluker and Catherine Tumber, 55–80. Boston: Beacon Press.

———. 2003. "The Negro Spiritual Speaks of Life and Death." In *African American religious thought: An anthology*. 29–49. Louisville, Ky: Westminster John Knox Press.

Tonry, Michael, and David P. Farrington, eds. 2005. *Crime and Punishment in Western Countries, 1980–1999*. Chicago: University of Chicago Press.

Trevisan, Maria Carolina. 2015, March 15. "Os defensores do impeach-ment são brancos." *Journalistas Livres*.

Varella, Drauzio. 1999. *Estacão Carandiru*. São Paulo: Companhia das Letras.

Wacquant, Loïc. 2001. "Deadly Symbiosis: When Ghetto and Prison Meet and Mesh." *Punishment and Society* 3: 95–134.

———. 2003. "Towards a Dictatorship of the Poor? Notes on the Penalization of Poverty in Brazil." *Punishment and Society* 5(2): 197–206.

Weber, Max. 1968. *Economy and Society: An Outline of Interpretive Sociology*. New York: Bedminster Press.

———. 1904–1905 [1996]. *The Protestant Ethic and the Spirit of Capitalism*. Translated by Talcott Parsons (1930). Los Angeles: Roxbury.

———. 1922 [1991]. *The Sociology of Religion*. Translated by Ephraim Fischoff. Boston: Beacon.

Werneck, Antônio. 2010, February 11. ' "Masmorra Medieval': Carceragem da Polinter Registra 56,7 Graus." *Globo*.

Western, Bruce. 2006. *Punishment and Inequality in America*. New York: Russell Sage Foundation.

Wheeler, Joanna. 2003. "New Forms of Citizenship: Democracy, Family, and Community in Rio de Janeiro, Brazil." *Gender and Development* 11(3): 36–44.

White, Ahmed A. 2008. "The Concept of 'Less Eligibility' and the Social Function of Prison Violence in Class Society." *Buffalo Law Review* 56: 737–820.

Willems, Emilio. 1967. *Followers of the New Faith: Culture Change and the Rise of Protestantism in Brazil and Chile*. Nashville, TN: Vanderbilt University Press.

Winchester, Daniel. 2008. "Embodying the Faith: Religious Practice and the Making of a Muslim Moral Habitus." *Social Forces* 86(4): 1753–1780.

INDEX

CPSIA information can be obtained
at www.ICGtesting.com
Printed in the USA
LVHW091711050121
675673LV00011B/2709